TAKE BACK YOUR

# AUTHORITY

# TAKE BACK YOUR
# AUTHORITY

## KINGDOM KEYS TO OVERTHROWING
## THE POWERS OF DARKNESS

## ISAAC PITRE

DESTINY IMAGE® PUBLISHERS, INC.

P.O. Box 310, Shippensburg, PA 17257-0310

*"Promoting Inspired Lives."*

This book and all other Destiny Image and Destiny Image Fiction books are available at Christian bookstores and distributors worldwide.

For more information on foreign distributors, call 717-532-3040.

Reach us on the Internet: www.destinyimage.com.

ISBN 13 TP: 978-0-7684-6401-6

ISBN 13 eBook: 978-0-7684-6402-3

For Worldwide Distribution, Printed in the U.S.A.

5 / 23

# CONTENTS

# FOREWORD

When I first heard Isaac Pitre speak on taking back your authority, I knew that it needed to be put in book form. Therefore, I am delighted and honored to write this foreword.

Since I first read a small booklet by Kenneth Hagin on spiritual authority, my life was changed. Prior to that time, I ended many of my prayers with the tagline, "If it be your will." I had no idea that God's will was revealed through His word and that I had a part to play in seeing it done.

One can safely say that it is biblical to believe that through us understanding our spiritual authority in the earth through the name of Jesus, that we can, indeed, see God's will be done on earth as it is in Heaven. Isaac Pitre has done us the good service of giving us practical, scriptural principles to see just that happen.

He begins at the beginning, in the garden. He calls it the "garden theology." If we are going to be part of God's will being done on the earth, we must know that He already showed us and gave us a model of what this world looked like when it was created. It could be said that earth was a colony of Heaven before the fall.

Isaac expounds in an exemplary way, that after the fall, satan's battle with you and me in the earth realm is over authority. He wanted authority in Heaven, and was kicked out, and then God created humankind and gives us what satan wanted! God gave his children dominion, and it was to be exercised over everything He created.

We all know that humankind fell into sin and needed a redeemer. Isaac writes of the mystery of Jesus; the redeemer, who came to forgive our sin and get His children's authority back for them.

Such a sacrifice surely is worthy of us using His Name to see salvation come to the world. Isaac puts it well when he says, "Jesus came to earth to reveal to humankind our identity, authority, and glory and to restore it back to us." Essentially, the same power that raised Jesus Christ from the dead dwells in us! Amazing!

I think with all of this, we need to learn to exercise just such authority! You are not meant to live a defeated life! We are called to be the head and not the tail. The tail just gets dragged around!

*Take Back Your Authority* is a must read for every believer. What a wondrous revelation to know that we can learn to function as the overcomers our Father created us to be! If you want to walk in victory, defeat the devil, win over sickness, fear, and a powerless life, continue to read! If you already are convinced that God does want His will to be done on earth as it is in Heaven, learning to skillfully use what Jesus gave us as our inheritance is a must!

CINDY JACOBS
Generals International
Dallas, Texas

# CHAPTER 1

# A Garden Theology

I t is my sincere belief that if we are ever going to walk in the true identity, authority, and victory that Christ has paid for us to live in, we need to have what I call a garden theology. You may ask, "What is a garden theology?" A garden theology is a revelation and understanding that everything that happened and transpired in the garden of Eden was God's perfect will for all of humankind. The reason we must understand this is because once God sets a truth into motion, He never changes His mind! That's why the scripture declares in Numbers 23:19: *"God is not a man, that He should lie, nor a son of man, that He should repent,"* or change His mind! What God sets into motion stays in motion until it is accomplished or finished! And Genesis 1 and 2 show us the perfect will of God.

As we began to look deeply into the plan that God created in the garden, we need to comprehend that what we see here is not just God's plan for Adam and Eve, but rather God's plan for humankind. That's why I titled this chapter "A Garden Theology." What God established in the garden should be the basis for our theology. Why? Because everything about the Bible and what we read in scripture is to get humankind and planet earth back to the original plan and purpose laid out in Genesis 1 and 2. I like to say it this way—until you understand Genesis, you will never truly understand Jesus! As we will discover later in this book, everything about Jesus is about Genesis. The whole reason

Jesus came was to rescue the plan that God established in the earth in Genesis. If there wasn't first a garden, there would be no need for a cross. Therefore, the apex of our theology is not the cross, but rather the garden. Everything Jesus did on the cross was to fix what Adam did in the garden! So before we discuss Jesus any further, let's first dive a little deeper into this garden theology.

## Until you understand Genesis, you will never truly understand Jesus!

*In the beginning God created the heavens and the earth. The earth was without form, and void; and darkness was on the face of the deep. And the Spirit of God was hovering over the face of the waters* (Genesis 1:1-2).

Let's stop right here at these first two verses, because I feel there is something very significant that needs to be pointed out, called the gap theory. The gap theory, in short, is the belief that something happened between Genesis 1:1 and Genesis 1:2. That in Genesis 1:1 God is creating the earth. In Genesis 1:2 God is rearranging an earth already created. Genesis 1:2 describes an earth that is waste, purposeless, and dark. It is clear by numerous scriptures that God did not create the earth this way. One of the scriptures can be found in Isaiah 45:18, which declares:

> *For thus says the Lord, who created the heavens, who is God, who formed the earth and made it, who has established it, who did not create it in vain, who formed it to be inhabited: "I am the Lord, and there is no other."*

By this one scripture alone, something had to happen to planet earth for it to become uninhabitable. While my assignment in this book is not to debate creationism, I only bring this up so that we can clearly understand the dominion mandate for humankind! It was for this purpose that God created humans. After God rearranged the earth in Genesis 1, He needed a ruler to set over the earth realm. Why, might you ask? Because of the judgment that came on planet earth because of the first ruler.

Jesus declared in Luke 10:18 that He beheld satan fall like lightning out of Heaven. Then we understand by Revelation 12:4 that when satan was cast down, he was cast down to earth. Most scholars believe, as do I, that lucifer at least had some form of rulership over this earth realm but was not satisfied to be a ruler over the earth with God and for God; he wanted to be a ruler in Heaven as one equal with God. Because of this misguided purpose, he became condemned and dethroned from his position among the archangels and stripped of his authority over the earth realm.

Isaiah 14:12-17 gives us insight into just what happened as lucifer was thrown down. He was in contention with God over authority! Now this is probably one of the most important revelations that any human could discover—the fact that lucifer is after authority, and he wanted it in both realms. It wasn't enough to just rule over the earth realm; he also wanted Heaven.

This sadistic desire is still in satan's warped mind today. Just because he was cast out doesn't mean he doesn't still want this authority. That's why it's important for you to understand this revelation, because his battle with you and me in the earth realm is over authority. You see, in Jeremiah 4:23-27 the prophet recalls a time when the earth was formless and void and had no light. This is a reference to Genesis 1:2. He speaks of a time when everything was destroyed, and total darkness filled the earth. That was the exact same thing quoted in Genesis. What is different about Jeremiah's account versus Moses' account of the earth in the beginning is that Jeremiah explained that God did it out of His fierce anger!

# Satan's battle with you and me in the earth realm is over authority.

The question is, what could make God so angry that He would judge and destroy the very earth He created? The answer—the fall of lucifer. After the fall of lucifer, God stripped him of his authority to rule over the earth realm. Everything that was under his authority in the earth realm was thrown into utter chaos. Therefore, God condemned the earth and withdrew His light, and everything on earth was destroyed that day. What was left of earth was a dark, void, wasteful, uninhabited place. The reason you must know this is because everything between God, satan, and humanity is about who will have authority over this earth!

When God came back on the scene in Genesis 1:2, He was ready to start rearranging the earth back into divine order and perfection. Only this time God put another ruler over it! Wow! When God created lucifer, He gave him the responsibility of stewarding the earth under a heavenly order and culture. He was responsible for overseeing the extension of the Kingdom of Heaven over the earth, before his rebellion.

We know through fossils and many other scientific discoveries that some type of life form and social order was here on planet earth before Adam—that there was a pre-Adamic world. Therefore, there had to be a ruler over it. In Ezekiel 28:13, the prophet is speaking to the King of Tyre, who represents a spiritual ruler over that territory. The prophet declares that whoever this spiritual ruler is, he was also "in Eden, the garden of God." We need to comprehend this statement because there were only three people mentioned in the garden of Eden: Adam, Eve, and the serpent.

We know that the serpent had to be seduced by satan for the serpent to deceive Eve. After God rearranged the earth and created all the living creatures, the Lord declared everything good! Nothing on earth had any source of evil or wickedness in it. The only source of evil or wickedness left in this realm was satan. So the serpent had to be acting under the influence of satan. This one truth establishes the fact that satan was in the garden. The question is, why was he there? For one reason and one reason only. He wanted authority back in the earth realm.

Remember, God judged the earth in Genesis 1 because of the rebellion of lucifer. What is important to point out here is that when God cast satan back down to the earth and then stripped him of his position, the earth was left without a ruler over it. It was then that God made the most earth-shattering statement ever declared in the history of the created ages: *"Let Us make man in Our image, according to Our likeness; let them have dominion"* (Genesis 1:26). The horror satan must have felt when he heard those words. Remember it was satan, in all his pride, that declared, "I will ascend into Heaven and rule just like God," only to be cast out as fast as lightning back down to the earth in humiliation! As he fell back to earth, a place where he thought he still occupied authority, God stripped him of his authority, then flooded the earth and destroyed everything in it, only to start all over and give the authority over the earth (an authority satan once had) into the hands of this creation called man!

When you get this revelation deep within your spirit, you understand that satan's conflict with you is not just spiritual but territorial! He wants back what you have—authority over the earth! It is for this reason we went back to the beginning. In the creation of humankind, God was righting a wrong that happened on planet earth. He was restoring the heavenly order and Kingdom back to earth. It was, and is, and will forever be the plan for God to have "on earth as it is in Heaven."

Now we understand why the battle with satan is so intense. He hates us because we occupy the territory that was once under his control. He is hell-bent on getting it back. But there is also another reason he hates us. It is because we are everything that he ever wanted to be! He is jealous of the fact that God gave to us the very thing that got him kicked out of Heaven. Satan was thrown out of Heaven because he tried to ascend into a rank and existence that was forbidden to him. In Isaiah 14:12-15, it is clear that lucifer wanted God's likeness and authority, but he wasn't created to have it.

In Genesis 1:26-28, we see that God made man in a rank and authority superior to anything that He had created before. He created man in His image, likeness, and gave man His authority. It is very apparent to me that God's plan for man was to establish Heaven's likeness, culture, and way of life in the earth. It was God's plan for man to rule the earth as He Himself did in Heaven. Therefore, God put Heaven in his heart! This is what happened when God breathed into his nostrils and released His Spirit and nature into man. Now all Adam and Eve had to do was just breathe. That's all they had to do—just be! God had so filled them with His Spirit and mind that whatever they did was God-like.

## It was God's plan for man to rule the earth as He Himself did in Heaven. Therefore, God put Heaven in his heart!

God was so confident that the earth realm was in good hands that the Bible declares in Genesis 2:3 that God rested. As far as God was concerned, the restoration of planet earth was complete! What an awesome responsibility Adam and Eve had—to rid the earth of evil and extend the garden, the culture of Heaven, to the ends of the earth. However, you and I know that God's plan for humankind and the earth was wickedly disrupted. God gave the man one command, and that was not to eat off the tree in the midst of the garden. This tree was holy unto the Lord. The fruit of it belonged to God and God alone. Without getting bogged down in all the theological discussions of what this tree represented, the fact is that God commanded them not to eat of it and decreed that the day they did, they would die. Now, this death would not be immediately physical, but it would be immediately spiritual.

You and I know the tragedy. They ate of it, and they died. I am writing this book so that we would understand that everything Jesus Christ came to do on earth was to fix and reverse the effect of this fall. When Adam fell, everything under his dominion fell with him. The ramifications of Adam's spiritual death not only affected humanity but also creation itself. Now we understand why the earth has been groaning (see Romans 8:22-24). That's right! Not only was humankind hit with sin and the curse, but Adam also allowed sin and the curse into the whole earth.

How could He have done this? If you would go back to God's original plan, He said, *"Let Us make man in Our image, according to Our likeness; let them have dominion."* This dominion was to be exercised over the earth and everything God created. Adam and Eve were given the assignment to not only bring Heaven to the earth, but to also keep hell out of the earth. So when Adam vacated his position of authority in the earth realm by his rebellion against God, the earth was left without a ruler. This was when satan and all his demonic forces were given the freedom to move in the earth realm.

Now satan has regained authority and access to the earth realm. Not because it belongs to him or he has the authority to do so, but because Adam vacated his authority. Satan and his demonic kingdom filled the void. If you want to know how devastating this treason of Adam against God was, just consider that in Genesis 1, God spent the whole chapter restoring the earth to divine order and original glory because it was in total chaos, darkness, and destruction. It had become this way because of satanic activity. Remember, God did not create it that way. Now, through Adam's treason, the very agent that caused confusion, destruction, chaos, and disorder has been allowed freedom in the earth realm to bring the same destruction to the earth and humankind again. What a tragedy!

Now in the earth realm, humanity must deal with fallen nature and fallen spirits, all as a result of Adam's transgression. This was not God's original plan! God came into the garden in the cool of the evening and asked the resounding question, "Adam, where are you?" God asked Adam this question not because He didn't know where Adam was, but because He knew where Adam wasn't. The phrase the cool of the evening is the Hebrew word *ruach,* for "spirit, breath, or wind." That phrase can be translated, "God came in the spirit or breath." When He did, He could not find Adam because he was missing from that dimension. When Adam fell, he fell from the spiritual nature, life, and image of God. Although he was still a spirit being, his spirit had lost all the God-DNA that was breathed into him. He was in essence a dead man walking!

Now that humankind has lost God's image, they are easily manipulated by satan because human nature is virtually the same as lucifer's. Humankind has morphed into a carnal creature dominated by sin, satan, and their senses. Not only that, now the earth's atmosphere is completely permeated with demonic activity. The earth itself is contaminated. The glorious harmony that God established in Genesis has been altered.

I want you to fathom the fact that if Adam hadn't sinned, there would have never been a thunderstorm, tornado, hurricane, tsunami, or earthquake. All of this began because of the fall. God's plan for the earth looked as if it was altered forever, as if all of humanity would have to live in sin and satanic oppression for the duration of earth's existence. But God had a plan! This was not a backup plan or a plan B. This was a plan that was developed before the foundation of the world! Glory! I love the fact that God in all His omniscience is always ahead of the game. Just when satan thought that God's plan for humankind and the earth realm was lost forever, and just when he thought he would never have to submit again to humankind in the earth, God gave him a prophecy! He told the serpent to keep his head up, because there was a heel coming for his head and He wouldn't miss! God was about to introduce satan and the earth to the last Adam! That's right! Another would come to restore everything the first one allowed to be destroyed! Get ready! Jesus is coming!

# CHAPTER 2

# THE MYSTERY OF JESUS

Even though we are thousands of years after His resurrection and millennia into the church age, I've discovered that many people still do not truly understand who Jesus is. Many people recognize Jesus for what He did, and rightfully so! He truly did heal and deliver and set the world free through the redemption in His blood. But once again, all those things are what Jesus did. My question is, do you know who He is? For this purpose, Jesus asked His disciples in Matthew 16:13, "Who do men say that I am?" Jesus asked His disciples this question because, even though they had been with Him and seen all the things that He did, they still didn't know who He was. But then Peter received revelation from the Father and declared, "You are the Christ, the Son of the living God." Let's take some time to dissect this statement.

First, it is astounding that it would take a revelation from God to reveal who Jesus was. That should tell you that something deeper here needs to be unlocked and revealed. When Jesus asked His disciples, "Who do men say that I am?" the rumors were wild! They ranged from John the Baptist to Elijah. The reason they couldn't come up with an answer is because the people were trying to figure Him out in the light of the Old Covenant and through the understanding of previous patterns and prophets. So even though they saw the miracles and heard the teachings, they still had no clue who He was.

After asking, "Who do the people say that I am?" Jesus pivoted to the disciples and asked them if they knew. Even though they had spent approximately three years with Him, they still didn't know—because it was hidden in a mystery! No one knew! No one could know until it was time for it to be revealed, and now was the time. With a blast of revelation knowledge from Heaven, Peter declared a truth that had been hidden in a mystery from the foundation of the world. *"You are the Christ, the Son of the living God!"*

Wow, what a statement. What Peter declared was, "You are God's Son as a man!" No one had ever seen a son of God as a man. And that was what Jesus came to reveal. Sonship! When Jesus asked His disciples who people said He was, some went back as far as Elijah. But to really understand Jesus they needed to keep going further back—all the way back to Adam! Adam was the original son of God as a man! We were just never able to see him or touch him. Now you understand why in 1 Corinthians 15:45, Paul called Jesus the "last Adam." The last one restored everything that the first one lost, and one of the things that the first Adam lost was the image and likeness of God and the ability to walk in dominion over the earth realm.

This was the purpose for which Jesus came, and this answers the question of who He was—He was the reintroduction of man into the earth as the offspring of Heaven! Glory! Now I think you can fully comprehend the statement I'm about to make. After Peter said, *"You* are the Christ, the Son of the living God," Jesus answered and said, *"You are Peter, and on this rock I will build My church"* (Matthew 16:18). Let's stop and just dissect this. What rock? Jesus meant that upon this massive revelation and foundation He would build His church. Are you ready? This phrase means "out of this truth you will be formed." The church is to be built out of sons of God as men! Jesus wasn't coming to raise up a religious organization. Jesus was coming to establish an offspring of people on planet earth who would be born out of Heaven, and to restore the lost identity, authority, and glory of humankind! Hallelujah!

---

**Jesus wasn't coming to raise up a religious organization. Jesus was coming to establish an offspring of people on planet earth who would be born out of Heaven.**

---

This is who He was, and this is why He came—to show us our original identity! Then He put a redemptive plan together to give it back to us. He even goes further to say that when He released these sons and daughters into the earth realm the gates of hell would not prevail against them. *"And I will give you the keys of the kingdom of heaven, and whatever you bind on earth will be bound in heaven, and whatever you loose on earth will be loosed in heaven"* (Matthew 16:19). Jesus said when these sons were born, they were going to represent Heaven and all of its authority in the earth realm. That is why the Greek word for *church* here is *ekklesia*. It means "a called assembly of citizens whose role is to act as a governing body for policy and decision making." The church is not just an assembly on the street corner in some neighborhood or city. The church is the gathering of the sons of God in the earth who convene to handle Kingdom affairs in the earth. No wonder Jesus said in Luke 2:49: *"I must be about My Father's business."* The Son's assignment is to take care of the business of the Father. That's now the role of the church in the earth!

Now that you understand who Jesus is, let's substantiate it a little further. There is another passage of scripture that gives us further insight into the mystery of Jesus:

> *Let this mind be in you which was also in Christ Jesus, who, being in the form of God, did not consider it robbery to be equal with God, but made Himself of no reputation, taking the form of a bondservant, and coming in the likeness of men. And being found in*

*appearance as a man, He humbled Himself
and became obedient to the point of death,
even the death of the cross. Therefore God
also has highly exalted Him and given Him
the name which is above every name, that at
the name of Jesus every knee should bow, of
those in heaven, and of those on earth, and of
those under the earth, and that every tongue
should confess that Jesus Christ is Lord, to the
glory of God the Father* (Philippians 2:5-11).

This passage is loaded with revelation about the divinity and humanity of Jesus. First, the scripture declares that Jesus was in the form of God but "did not consider it robbery to be equal with God." That verse means that even though He was equal with God, when it came time to give up that equality, He didn't feel as though He was robbed or stolen from. He gladly gave up His position and took on the level of a bondservant and came in the likeness of men. Wow! That means when we see Jesus in the earth, we are seeing Him in a lower form. He previously existed in a higher form with the Father. It's clear that He had to give up equality with God to become a man. It's stunning to think that He who made humans now had to demote Himself and become like the creatures He made!

This is what the scripture means by "He humbled Himself." The Creator had to become what He created in order to redeem humanity. This shows you how far He was willing to go to redeem you and me. Then the scripture declares that He was *"found in appearance as a man"* and that He became obedient to the point of death, even the death of the cross. It's important to note that Jesus wasn't just obedient to the Father, although He was. He was also obedient to the assignment. I bring out these points to reveal to you that Jesus Christ didn't come to the earth in the fullness of God! He stripped Himself of that. He came to earth in the fullness of man in the image of God! That's what He wanted the earth to see. No one had ever seen a man in the image of God before. In order to see a man in the image of God you would need to have seen Adam before the fall. But the last Adam came to reveal to humankind and the earth realm what a son of God looks like as a man.

In John 1:14, the scripture declares, *"The Word became flesh and dwelt among us, and we beheld His glory, the glory as of the only begotten of the Father, full of grace and truth."* John declares that when we saw Jesus, we were beholding a Man begotten of the Father. God's Son in the flesh! Whew! Once again, I am emphasizing the fact that Jesus had to step down, way down, in class, rank, authority, and glory to become a man. And even though He was in a lower class of existence in the earth than He had in Heaven, He was still the highest-ranking being in the earth realm. He was the Man of men. One more scripture that gives more clarity to this truth is found in John 17:1-5:

*Jesus spoke these words, lifted up His eyes to heaven, and said: "Father, the hour has come. Glorify Your Son, that Your Son also may glorify You, as You have given Him authority over all flesh, that He should give eternal life to as many as You have given Him. And this is eternal life, that they may know You, the only true God, and Jesus Christ whom You have sent. I have glorified You on the earth. I have finished the work which You have given Me to do. And now, O Father, glorify Me together with Yourself, with the glory which I had with You before the world was."*

The question is this. If Jesus was asking for the glory that He had with the Father before the world was, what glory did He have on earth? If He's asking for something back, He must have lost it or been stripped of it. Once again, this goes back to Philippians 2:5-11. It is clear that Jesus had to strip Himself of the fullness of the glory that He had with God and humble Himself to come in the fullness of humanity. But now, He said the hour had come for the great exchange. What is the great exchange? The great exchange is what happened on the cross. The whole Bible is about God's plan for humanity. God created the man in His image and likeness and gave him dominion. Adam lost this image, likeness, and dominion, and God had a plan to get it back. Numbers 23:19 says:

*God is not a man, that He should lie, nor a son of man, that He should repent. Has He said, and will He not do? Or has He spoken, and will He not make it good?*

Just to clarify—once God sets something into motion or establishes a purpose, He doesn't change His mind. God had a plan for humanity, and even what Adam did could not and would not stop it! In response to what Adam did, in the fullness of time Jesus stripped Himself of all heavenly glory and humbled Himself to become a Man in order to restore the original glory, dignity, honor, and authority back to humankind.

By the way, the word for *glory* is the Greek word *doxa*. In this verse it means "honor and dignity." So when we see Jesus in the earth, we are not seeing Him in all of His heavenly glory; He emptied Himself of that. We are seeing Him in all of our glory! Meaning humankind! That's right! Jesus came to earth to reveal to humankind our identity, authority, and glory and to restore it back to us.

Jesus then declared in John 17:5, *"And now, O Father, glorify Me together with Yourself, with the glory which I had with You before the world was."* In other words, "Now that I have paid the price to give humanity their glory back, I want My glory back!" What an awesome exchange! Jesus stepped down from His position to come to change our condition. Then once He fixed our condition, He stepped back up to His position! Now everything has been recovered and restored in Christ, and God can begin the process of renewing His master plan in the earth through humankind. However, Jesus' death, burial, and resurrection were not the end of the Master's plan. In many ways, it was just the beginning! You may ask, "Didn't Jesus pay it all and finish the work of redemption?" My answer would be emphatically yes! But Jesus' death was more than the just the ending of sin—it was also the beginning of sons! Now that we can be born again, a new race of people can experience a level of sonship with the Father in the earth. This was the main purpose for which Jesus came to earth!

## Jesus came to earth to reveal to humankind our identity, authority, and glory and to restore it back to us.

Romans 8:29 says, *"For whom He foreknew, He also predestined to be conformed to the image of His Son, that He might be the firstborn among many brethren."* Jesus did not come to be the only one; He came to be the first one among many others. God was after His original plan for humanity that He purposed in Adam—sons and daughters in His image and likeness. That's why Jesus came to demonstrate and break the power of sin and satan over our lives. We were never created to have sin and wickedness in us. We were supposed to be His offspring. When you see Jesus in the earth realm, you are looking at the true potential of God's seed as a Man.

It is important that you clearly realize this revelation of the mystery of Jesus. Now that you clearly understand who He was, you should also be able to clearly understand who you are, because that's what Jesus came to reveal to humankind. I call it modeling the glory. You see, before Jesus redeemed humanity, He showed what a redeemed Man looked like. I like to say it this way: "When I look at Jesus, I see my potential." Jesus showed me the true identity and authority of what a human born of God could do and be in the earth.

It's important that you understand that everything Jesus did in the earth, He had to do within the parameters that God established for humanity. God said, "Let man have dominion." It would have been illegal for Jesus to do anything outside of the jurisdiction God had designed for humanity. So everything Jesus did, He did within the parameters and scope of the authority of a man! This is what was so confusing to people. From Nicodemus to Peter, they all knew that He was a man; they just didn't know what kind of man He was! What they didn't realize, until Peter received the revelation, was that He was a man in the image and likeness of God with dominion in the earth to execute Heaven's will.

One the reasons we visited John 17:1-5 was to see that when Jesus functioned in the earth, He functioned in a glory, rank, honor, dignity, and authority that didn't originally belong to Him. It originally belonged to Adam. Remember, He had to humble Himself to wear that demoted level of dignity and authority, according to Philippians 2:5-8. Therefore, it is astounding to realize that when you see all the miracles, signs, and wonders that Jesus performed, He says, "That is not even My glory—that's humanity's. I had to stoop way low to put this glory on!" Wow! Therefore, Jesus' message to us is, "I did not come to be celebrated. I came to be duplicated! The glory I had in the earth was yours, and I died to give it back to you! So wear it!"

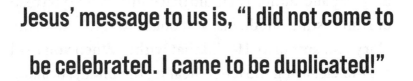

# Jesus' message to us is, "I did not come to be celebrated. I came to be duplicated!"

It's time for the church to rise up as sons and daughters and walk in the identity, dignity, and authority Christ died to restore to us. This will revolutionize your life and totally change the way you read Matthew, Mark, Luke, and John. Now when you read about Jesus in the

Gospels, you will do so with the understanding that He was revealing your true identity and authority. Therefore, He declared in John 14:12: *"Most assuredly, I say to you, he who believes in Me, the works that I do he will do also; and greater works than these he will do, because I go to My Father."* Jesus said we would do the same works because when He did the works He did them with the same authority God gave to humanity. In other words, these are the works that redeemed people have the authority to do! Jesus simply came into the earth and picked up the lost authority and assignment given to Adam and completely fulfilled it. Then, He turned around and handed that assignment to the church—the born offspring of God.

Going forward, when you read the Gospels about Christ, you need to do so with this mindset. When you read of Jesus healing the sick, you ought to say, "That's my glory and authority He did that with!" When you read of Him casting out devils, you ought to say, "That's my glory and authority He did that with!" When you read of Him cleansing the leper, healing the blind, speaking to the storm, walking on the water, or even raising the dead, you ought to say, "That's my glory and authority He did that with!"

The mystery of Jesus is revealed in the clear truth that the Last Adam walked the earth not to just restore what the first Adam lost, but also who the first Adam lost—a kind of people in the earth realm that reveal the character, nature, and authority of God. First John 3:2 says it best: *"Beloved, now we are children of God; and it has not yet been revealed what we shall be, but we know that when He is revealed, we shall be like Him, for we shall see Him as He is."* I don't know if any of us will truly reach the full potential and glory of who we have been created to be on this side of Heaven, but I do know that we owe it to Jesus and the Father to chase after it.

According to scripture, there is one more mystery that needs to be revealed in the earth in order to complete the assignment of God through Christ. It is found in Colossians 1:26-27:

> *The mystery which has been hidden from ages and from generations, but now has been revealed to His saints. To them God willed to make known what are the riches of the glory of this mystery among the Gentiles: which is Christ in you, the hope of glory.*

Wow! Paul said that the mystery of all mysteries was not just how God was going to become a Man in Christ, but rather how God was going to get Christ in you! The mission is not complete until the mystery of who Jesus was is revealed in who we are in Him and He in us! So let us live our lives to become the revealers of the mystery!

# CHAPTER 3

# THE DOCTRINE OF SONSHIP

As we peer into the mystery a little further, we discover the doctrine of sonship. The doctrine of sonship is the revelation that salvation in Christ Jesus not only changed my spiritual condition, but it also changed my spiritual position. I am not just a saint; I'm also a son! Salvation is not complete until I get my condition and position restored. This authority that we are taking back will not be completely realized until we get an understanding of who we are and where we are in Christ. That's right, when you got born again your position shifted. You are not who you used to be, and you're not where you used to be. You have been shifted positionally.

The reason I'm driving this point home is because you can't have dominion until you understand where dominion comes from. Dominion comes from placement! Dominion is authority, and authority is a product of placement. In other words, authority works by positioning! The weight of authority you carry depends on how you are positioned with the One who authorized you. The centurion understood this in Matthew 8:5-13. We will talk about this more extensively in Chapter 5, but the unique revelation the centurion had was a revelation of authority! He declared that he was a man under authority and a man in authority, which is how authority works. The authority he had came from who he was under.

This why a revelation of your position in Christ is so important. When Jesus rose from the dead, He declared all authority in Heaven and earth was given to Him. That means He's the author of authority. No one is over Him! No one outranks Him! No one can dispute Him. He holds the highest authority possible. This is important to grasp because He took His authority and delegated it to you and me! He is the one we are under! I cannot express to you enough how important it is for us to receive this truth, because all that we have in Christ will never be appropriated if we are out of position.

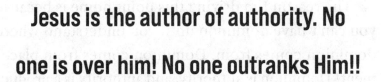

# Jesus is the author of authority. No one is over him! No one outranks Him!!

Let's delve deeper into just how we obtained such authority with Christ. Remember, when Adam fell in the garden, what God lost was not a religion or a belief system. What God lost were sons and daughters after His kind! It was always God's plan to let the kids rule the earth. His kids and His kind! That's why God gave Adam and Eve dominion. It is because dominion is the birthright of the kids! Authority belongs to the family, and the extension of the rule of God in the earth was to be enforced and released through His seed—Adam and Eve. When they sinned in the garden, they lost this right to rule and govern. Because dominion belongs only to the offspring of God, if humankind is ever going to have dominion again, they need to become sons and daughters again. Only those who bear His image are authorized to rule.

With this clarity, now you understand the complete mission of the Messiah. It is to restore sonship and rulership to humankind. As we see how Jesus functioned in the earth realm, it is clear that one of His assignments was to demonstrate the level of sonship and rulership that we possessed with the Father. And oh my, did He demonstrate it! Let's look at one occasion in the life of Jesus when His authority was on full display.

In Matthew 8:23-27, we have perhaps the most powerful demonstration of the authority of Jesus ever mentioned in scripture. Jesus and the disciples were on a boat traveling to the other side of the sea when a great storm arose. Jesus was at the bottom of the ship asleep. When the storm became more violent and water began to fill the boat, the disciples panicked and woke Jesus up. Jesus then went to the edge of the boat and did something no other man had ever done before—He spoke to the storm! He commanded the storm to cease by declaring peace to the wind and "be still" to the waves. And there was a great calm. After the seas were calmed, His disciples murmured among themselves, *"What manner of man is this, that even the winds and the sea obey him"* (Matthew 8:27 KJV).

Wow. The question was one of great revelation. In essence, they were saying, "We know He is a Man, we just don't know what kind of Man He is." Jesus did things no other man had ever done. This is what Jesus came to reveal to them—the authority that a son of God has over the earth. Jesus displayed a scope of authority that was unprecedented. This Man didn't just speak to men, He spoke to wind, and it obeyed! The wind responded to His authority!

The reason I took the time in Chapter 2 to explain the mystery of Jesus was because I wanted to reveal the fact that everything that Jesus did while He was on the earth, He had to do it as a Man. He showed humanity the extent of the authority they could exercise over the earth as sons and daughters of God. Not only did Jesus display this sonship to them, but He also invited them to partake of it. Ultimately, He knew the authority that He possessed would one day be theirs!

I could spend the rest of this book taking you through scripture after scripture in the Gospels where Jesus manifested this kind of authority over everything from sickness to satan. But my point in this chapter is to get you to focus more on why and how He did what He did, instead of what He did. He did it because He was a Son. That's why the doctrine of sonship is so crucial. Let me be clear—Jesus is the Savior. But if we treat Him like our Savior only, He stays detached from us. When we see

Him also as a son, He becomes a part of us! As Romans 8:29 declares, He is *"the firstborn among many brethren"* (KJV). While Jesus was on the earth, He was the only one. But after the resurrection, He became the first one. That's the revelation in this chapter: Jesus' assignment was to bring us into sonship! Now that we have been redeemed by His blood, according to Romans 8:15, we are no longer slaves; we are sons!

---

## Jesus is the Savior. But if we treat Him like our Savior only, He stays detached from us. When we see Him also as a son, He becomes a part of us!

---

With this understanding, it is evident that salvation changed my status. I have been changed conditionally and positionally. I'm now an heir of God and a joint heir with Christ (see Romans 8:14-17). I must begin to renew my mind to this reality. Now that I'm a son, I have been granted all the rank, rights, and privileges that come with that position. One of the main privileges is authority in and over the earth realm. That's why satan was so horrified after the resurrection. First Corinthians 2:8 declares that had the rulers of this age known, they would not have crucified Him.

One of the main reasons the enemy inspired men to remove Jesus from the earth was because of the authority He displayed. Satan knew he had to get this authority out of the way in order to rule. Imagine the horror when satan discovered that after the resurrection, he hadn't removed Jesus or His authority—he multiplied it! When Jesus arose with all authority given to Him in Heaven and earth (see Matthew 28:18), it gave Him the right to delegate that authority to everyone who would believe on Him and be born again! Now that authority on earth belongs to and has been given to the children of God. Our assignment on earth is to do with it what He did with it—bring the Kingdom of Heaven to the earth! This why position is so important. We have been placed in a position of authority by birth. We are born to rule. That's exactly right! Rulership was the first Adam's purpose and rulership is the last Adam's purpose.

Until we see ourselves as sons of God, we will never stand in our rightful position to release our authority, because our authority comes from the position. Ephesians 2:1-6 reveals to us our true position as children of God:

> *And you He made alive, who were dead in trespasses and sins, in which you once walked according to the course of this world, according to the prince of the power of the air, the*

*spirit who now works in the sons of dis-
obedience, among whom also we all once
conducted ourselves in the lusts of our flesh,
fulfilling the desires of the flesh and of the
mind, and were by nature children of wrath,
just as the others.*

*But God, who is rich in mercy, because of His
great love with which He loved us, even when
we were dead in trespasses, made us alive
together with Christ (by grace you have been
saved), and raised us up together, and made us
sit together in the heavenly places in Christ Jesus.*

# Until we see ourselves as sons of God, we will never stand in our rightful position to release our authority.

"Seated in heavenly places" is a position we occupy
with Christ. Remember, we are joint heirs with Christ—
we occupy the same position with the Father that Christ
occupies. And Christ occupies that position because He

is a son. So are we! Hebrews 2:10-11 clearly states that the purpose for salvation was to bring many sons to glory:

> For it was fitting for Him, for whom are all things and by whom are all things, in bringing many sons to glory, to make the captain of their salvation perfect through sufferings. For both He who sanctifies and those who are being sanctified are all of one, for which reason He is not ashamed to call them brethren.

The phrase "captain of our salvation" is very telling. The word for *captain* is the Greek word *archēgos*. *Archē* means 1) beginning, origin; 2) the person or thing that commences, the first person or a thing in a series. *Gos* means "one who takes the lead and thus affords an example, a predecessor in a matter, pioneer." When you understand the meaning of this word *archēgos*, it is clear that Jesus came to be the predecessor, pioneer, and prototype of a new kind of people. He would be the first in a series to come! Whew! He wanted to bring many sons into sonship. Once this gets down into our hearts, we will understand why He said in John 14:12:

> Most assuredly, I say to you, he who believes in Me, the works that I do he will do also; and greater works than these he will do, because I go to My Father.

This phrase "go to My Father" has the same meaning He unveiled in John 14:2-3. He was telling them, "I'm going to prepare a place for you with the Father, and that place is not just Heaven." Thank God for Heaven. But you won't be doing "greater works" there. He is talking about doing something with the Father that will assist you while you are here on earth. He is telling them, "I'm going to bring you into a position with the Father. I'm going to bring you into the family. And when I do, the authority that I have, you will have also."

The position of sonship gave them the authority and right to do the work that the Father sent them to do. It is clear that the terminology "captain of salvation" means the beginner and originator of a particular saved race and kind of people. This means it would start with Him but would be finished and carried on by the ones coming behind Him. I suggest that you and I get in line! When a car or some product comes off the assembly line, the cars that come off the line are exact replicas of the prototype. The prototype is just the first. But it is not the only! Remember that Jesus is the firstborn among many brethren. You and I are born again with no less privilege and position than the prototype. This authority and inheritance that we possess is the exact same authority as the captain of our salvation.

The plan of the Father was to start a duplication process in the earth. First, we would duplicate the image. Then we would duplicate the likeness. After that we would duplicate the dominion. And the earth would be filled with the reproductions of Christ through the church. This was a master plan. The goal was to keep producing these models of Christ to continue rolling off the assembly line of Heaven until the whole earth was filled with His glory. Hebrews 2:10 reveals that this is the glory that God wants to bring us into. It is the glory of the prototype. Therefore, it is so crucial that we begin to put major emphasis on the doctrine of sonship. It is clear that it was not only God's will to save us from eternal damnation, but also to transform us into the image of His Son and give us the same rights and privileges as a son that Jesus possessed. And one of the main privileges was authority!

I will expound on this more in the next chapter. When we talk about sonship, I want to implore you to remember it is your spirit that this sonship is conferred upon. I like to call it your born identity! If you only focus on the natural, you will never look like a son or feel like a son. It is your spirit that makes you a son. It was born of and from your Father. As this becomes more real to you, you will begin to see yourself from a spiritual perspective. Once that starts to happen, your faith will arise because you realize this position was given to your spirit and has nothing to do with the natural. *"Therefore, if anyone is in Christ, he is a new creation; old things have passed away; behold, all things have become new"* (2 Corinthians 5:17). We now understand what part of us was passed away and what part of us was made new. It was our spirit. Now our spirits become the source for our identity and authority. So let us learn how to live in our born-again identity!

# CHAPTER 4

# THE POWER OF HIS RESURRECTION

n Philippians 3, the apostle Paul lays out a revelation that I would like to discuss further in this chapter:

> But what things were gain to me, these I have counted loss for Christ. Yet indeed I also count all things loss for the excellence of the knowledge of Christ Jesus my Lord, for whom I have suffered the loss of all things, and count them as rubbish, that I may gain Christ and be found in Him, not having my own righteousness, which is from the law, but that which is through faith in Christ, the righteousness which is from God by faith; that I may know Him and the power of His resurrection, and the fellowship of His sufferings, being conformed to His death, if, by any means, I may attain to the resurrection from the dead.
>
> Not that I have already attained, or am already perfected; but I press on, that I may lay hold of that for which Christ Jesus has also laid hold of me. Brethren, I do not count myself to have apprehended; but one thing I do, forgetting those things which are behind and reaching forward to those things which are ahead, I press toward the goal for the prize of the upward call of God in Christ Jesus.
>
> Therefore let us, as many as are mature, have this mind; and if in anything you think

*otherwise, God will reveal even this to you. Nevertheless, to the degree that we have already attained, let us walk by the same rule, let us be of the same mind* (Philippians 3:7-16).

The apostle's statement *"that I may know Him and the power of His resurrection"* should become the cry of every believer. The revelation in these passages gives us insight into the Father's desire for those who believe in Him. You cannot really reclaim your victory over the enemy until you understand how Jesus won it. It is His victory that He gives to you and me. Therefore, I say reclaim it, because you already have it! The difference between the resurrection of Jesus and all other resurrections is that all other resurrections were only physical. Men and women died physically and were raised again physically. But Jesus' resurrection wasn't just physical. It was also spiritual! That's what separates His resurrection from all others. Many people in the Old and New Testament had come back from the physical death. But no one had ever come back from spiritual death.

As we previously saw, after Adam sinned in the garden, all humankind experienced spiritual death. Our spirits literally died. We were still living souls, just with dead spirits. Having lost God's nature and character, all of humankind was in a death existence until Christ. Even though God used many men and women in the Bible, they were all still spiritually unregenerate men and women. He used them because he could put His Spirit upon them. But He could not put His Spirit within them. John said in John 1:33:

> *I did not know Him, but He who sent me to baptize with water said to me, "Upon whom you see the Spirit descending, and remaining on Him, this is He who baptizes with the Holy Spirit."*

Up until Christ, no one had the capacity to house the Spirit of God within them because of spiritual death. But God had told John that He would be able to recognize the one whom the Father sent by recognizing the one in whom the Holy Spirit could live. When John saw the Spirit remain, he knew that Jesus was the one.

What gave Jesus the capacity to house the Holy Spirit? It was the fact that His Spirit was alive and not dead. His Spirit was in the image and likeness of God, which gave Him the capacity to be filled with the Holy Spirit. If we understand this clearly, we will catch a glimpse of what a resurrected life should look like in the believer. Jesus declared something in John 11 that I'm not sure many people hearing Him that day understood:

> *So when Jesus came, He found that he had already been in the tomb four days. Now Bethany was near Jerusalem, about two miles away. And many of the Jews had joined the women around Martha and Mary, to comfort them concerning their brother.*

> *Then Martha, as soon as she heard that Jesus*
> *was coming, went and met Him, but Mary*
> *was sitting in the house. Now Martha said*
> *to Jesus, "Lord, if You had been here, my*
> *brother would not have died. But even now*
> *I know that whatever You ask of God, God*
> *will give You."*
>
> *Jesus said to her, "Your brother will rise*
> *again."*
>
> *Martha said to Him, "I know that he will rise*
> *again in the resurrection at the last day."*
>
> *Jesus said to her, "I am the resurrection and*
> *the life. He who believes in Me, though he*
> *may die, he shall live"* (John 11:17-25).

When Martha heard this, she was only thinking of a natural resurrection. But Jesus was talking about a whole other revelation. When He spoke the words *"I am the resurrection and the life,"* He was declaring a few things. He was trying to reveal to her that He had power over natural death and natural life. Before, He raised the widow's son at Nain (see Luke 7:11-17). Even though this resurrection was miraculous, it was still only a physical resurrection. We see again the display of His mighty authority when He raised Jairus' daughter in Luke 8:40-56.

> *But He put them all outside, took her by the*
> *hand and called, saying, "Little girl, arise."*
> *Then her spirit returned, and she arose*
> *immediately. And He commanded that she*

*be given something to eat. And her parents were astonished, but He charged them to tell no one what had happened* (Luke 8:54-56).

What an incredible display of His authority again! However, it was still only a physical resurrection from the dead.

What Jesus was trying to convey to Martha was the fact that not only was He the One sent to cause resurrections, but He was the resurrection and the life. He Himself would become a resurrected being who would bring life not only physically but spiritually! Therefore, the words, "He that believes in me shall never die," address more than just existing eternally forever without physical death. It means existing eternally forever without spiritual death. Remember, everyone is going to live forever in eternity, whether you're saved or not. Spirits do not die or cease to exist. You simply must determine where you are going to live—in Heaven or in hell. However, the resurrection Jesus referred to would change human history forever.

It's fascinating to think of the events that unfolded when Jesus was on the cross and in the heart of the earth for three days and nights. What was happening was such a mystery that the Bible declares had the princes of this world known about it, they wouldn't have crucified Him (see 1 Corinthians 2:6-8). Jesus left them a hint in John 12:24, but because they were only thinking naturally, they didn't have the wisdom to discern it. He states:

*Most assuredly, I say to you, unless a grain of wheat falls into the ground and dies, it remains alone; but if it dies, it produces much grain.*

# If you want to get rid of a seed, the last thing you would ever do is put it in the ground!

If they would have known this, they certainly wouldn't have crucified and buried Him. If you want to get rid of a seed, the last thing you would ever do is put it in the ground! Jesus' parable was about a revelation concerning the purpose of His death. He would die alone, but after that many would be brought to life! In order to bring many to life, Jesus would have to destroy the sin nature that was in humanity. In order to do this, He must become sin in order to pay the price for sinful humankind. One man got us in it, and one man had to bring us out of it.

*Therefore, just as through one man sin entered the world, and death through sin, and thus death spread to all men, because all sinned—(For until the law sin was in the world, but sin is not imputed when there is no law. Nevertheless death reigned from Adam to Moses, even over those who had not sinned according to the likeness of the transgression of Adam, who is a type of Him who was to come. But the free gift is not like the offense. For if by the one man's offense many died, much more the grace of God and the gift by the grace of the one Man, Jesus Christ, abounded to many. And the gift is not like that which came through the one who sinned. For the judgment which came from one offense resulted in condemnation, but the free gift which came from many offenses resulted in justification. For if by the one man's offense death reigned through the one, much more those who receive abundance of grace and of the gift of righteousness will reign in life through the One, Jesus Christ.)*

*Therefore, as through one man's offense judgment came to all men, resulting in condemnation, even so through one Man's righteous act the free gift came to all men, resulting in justification of life. For as by one man's disobedience many were made sinners, so also by one Man's obedience many will be made righteous* (Romans 5:12-19).

That which came through Adam resulted in spiritual death, but that which came through Christ resulted in spiritual life. Jesus went after the sin nature. This was why John declared in John 1:29: *"The next day John saw Jesus coming toward him, and said, 'Behold! The Lamb of God who takes away the sin of the world!'"* This is how Jesus took away the sin of the world—by destroying the sin nature and its grip on humanity. Jesus did not come to just remove us from the penalty of sin; He also came to remove us from the nature of sin. It was the resurrection that did this.

As Jesus hung on the cross, 2 Corinthians 5:21 gives us insight into exactly what was going on: *"For He made Him who knew no sin to be sin for us, that we might become the righteousness of God in Him."* On the cross, Jesus received within Himself the sin nature in all its fullness and became a sinner! I believe the statement made on the cross in Luke 23:46 was the greatest statement of faith and trust ever uttered in human history:

> *When Jesus had cried out with a loud voice, He said, "Father, 'into Your hands I commit My spirit.'" Having said this, He breathed His last.*

He had to trust that the Father would bring His Spirit back to life again. As Jesus gave up the ghost and died, it was not just a natural death. We were beholding the spiritual death of a Man who was born with spiritual life. The sentence given to pay the price was three days and three nights in the heart of the earth. Matthew 12:40 says, *"For as Jonah was three days and three nights in the belly of the great fish, so will the Son of Man be three days and three nights in the heart of the earth."* There, God the Father displayed the greatest demonstration of His power ever revealed to principalities and powers and humankind. He recreated a human spirit!

No one had ever conquered spiritual death. No spirit being had ever died and come back to life. Many physical beings had been raised from physical death, as I stated earlier. But spiritual death was undefeated! It held every man from Adam up to that moment. But Jesus, our Champion, was about to destroy hell's undefeated streak! After paying the price for spiritual death and meeting the demands required for justice, Jesus was about to introduce to principalities and powers something that would strip them of all power and authority over humankind. The new creation! Jesus, the firstborn from the dead!

Can you imagine what happened in hell at the sight of Jesus? He was not only resurrected from spiritual death, but He now had the authority to resurrect humanity from spiritual death. The right and authority to do this was given to Him by the Father, and the first place that Jesus exercised this authority wasn't even on earth—it was in the underworld. When He led captivity captive and preached to the spirits who were in prison.

> *But to each one of us grace was given according to the measure of Christ's gift. Therefore He says:*

> *"When He ascended on high, He led captivity captive, and gave gifts to men."*
> *(Now this, "He ascended"—what does it mean but that He also first descended into the lower parts of the earth? He who descended is also the One who ascended far above all the heavens, that He might fill all things)* (Ephesians 4:7-10).

After Jesus received this authority to give spiritual life, the Word declares that He used this authority in the lower parts of the earth. One of these places is believed to be "Abraham's bosom," spoken of in Luke 16:19-31. Abraham's bosom was a holding place for the departed spirits who were awaiting the promise of the Father. Many scholars believe that these were also the covenant people of God who were kept by Abraham's faith when he made covenant with God. I believe the scripture bears this out in Romans 4:3, *"For what does the Scripture say? 'Abraham believed God, and it was accounted to him for righteousness.'"* Even though Abraham was not spiritually righteous, the Word declares he was accounted righteous. This gave God the right to treat Abraham with covenant kindness. But even though Abraham was accounted righteous, the Bible still declares in Hebrews 11:13:

> *These all died in faith, not having received the promises, but having seen them afar off were assured of them, embraced them and*

*confessed that they were strangers and pilgrims on the earth.*

They were still waiting! I can see in my imagination Abraham and all of the spirits throughout the ages waiting and waiting for Jesus to come and make good on His promise. As time ticked on through the years, decades, and millennia, some of the spirits were constantly asking Abraham, "Are you sure He's coming?" And Abraham would reply, "I still believe He is!" Then suddenly, after 2,000-plus years and 42 generations, they saw a figure in the distance approaching them, shining and glowing like the noonday sun. They heard a sound that sounded like the clanging of keys. As He came closer, they realized it was Him, the One, the resurrected Son of the living God. Jesus then raised His voice and declared, "I am He who was dead, but now I'm alive forevermore!" Abraham looked around and shouted to everyone, "I told you He was coming!" And they shouted and rejoiced as they were led out of the underworld as resurrected, glorified spirits! The best part is that satan had to watch them go! There was nothing he or any principality or power could do about it! Spiritual death had been defeated and hell had been stripped of its authority. In one moment, Jesus defeated death, hell, and the grave.

I wanted to expound on the resurrection because without a spiritual understanding of it, you will never truly understand the power and authority that has been given to the new creation. The new birth is where we get all our rights and privileges from. Jesus did all that He did just to restore it all back to us. But we could not receive it or experience it while being spiritually dead. Therefore, through the resurrection, we have now been given the spiritual and legal right to seize authority in the spirit realm.

## Spiritual death had been defeated and hell had been stripped of its authority. In one moment, Jesus defeated death, hell, and the grave.

I want you to meditate on this thought: "The new creation is the highest-ranking spiritual class of being in the earth!" You and I are far above the rank, status, class, and authority that satan or any of his minions could ever dream to have. It is my spiritual status, not my natural status, that gives me the preeminence. Jesus went to hell and back to give us this position, and we dare not let hell defeat us now that we have it. As we thank God Almighty and glorify Jesus for all that was accomplished

in the resurrection, I want you to know that the resurrection was just the beginning. There is still one more
level I would like to explain to you to take you even further. After the resurrection, we have the ascension! Jesus
raised you up just to sit you down!

# CHAPTER 5

# SIT DOWN

**P**aul's phrase "seated together in heavenly places" in Ephesians 2:4-6 is one of the most powerful statements in all the Bible. This statement shows us the supremacy of our authority. This is why we can't preach the resurrection without the ascension. Both go together. The finished work of Christ ends with the ascension! Until Christ sat down at the right hand of the Father, the redemptive work of salvation was not completed. You and I were buried with Him in His death. We were raised with Him in His resurrection. The last phase is that we ascended with Him to sit in a place at the right hand of the Father in supreme authority.

My complete redemption is not consummated until I take my seat. I say it like this, "Until you take the blood and take your seat, you're not complete!" This is one of the most amazing revelations that we could ever possess as children of the Most High God. In fact, the church was born from God, not just to be receivers of great revelation. Ephesians 3:8-11 reveals to us that we are to be a great revelation. To whom are we a revelation, you might ask? To principalities and powers in heavenly places! That's right! God hid a mystery in you and me for an appointed time to be revealed to the devil and all of his hosts. The Word of God declares that the mystery of the church was from the beginning and had been hidden in God until the resurrection of Jesus Christ. It is clear that God was about to give birth to something in the earth realm, but also in the heavenly realm, which satan never saw coming. The church!

---

# Until you take the blood and take your seat, you're not complete!

---

The body of Christ is what God wanted revealed to the principalities and powers in heavenly places! The church, not just Jesus, would be placed in authority in a realm over the earth. When Jesus rose from the dead, He upgraded the church's authority. When God created Adam and Eve, He gave them authority over the earth. But when Jesus arose, He received authority in Heaven and on earth. This was an extension of authority Adam and Eve never had. Then, according to Ephesians 1:22-23: *"And He put all things under His feet, and gave Him to be head over all things to the church, which is His body, the fullness of Him who fills all in all."*

Now the function of this authority is extended not just on earth, but over everything from Heaven to earth. This was a revelation to the principalities and powers in heavenly places because they knew Jesus had this kind of rule and authority, but they didn't expect the church to have this kind of rule and authority. Imagine their surprise when Christ sat down at the right hand of God, and they saw us sit down with Him. It is this seated position that the body of Christ functions from—a position far above principalities and powers. But just because we have authority, that doesn't mean we will automatically have victory. Why? Because satan is an outlaw! He doesn't respect authority. We must enforce it. Satan didn't respect God's position, so you know he doesn't respect yours. That's why we must stand our ground. Ephesians 6:10-18 tells us that we are in a spiritual battle. Spiritual battles are not won with bullets and guns. Spiritual battles are won with spiritual authority and power. They are won when someone who is in authority declares the word of God, forcing demonic principalities to submit. Therefore, Jesus said in Mark 16:17, *"They will cast out demons."* It is because our assignment as the church is to control and patrol the heavenly places. If we control the heavens, the earth will line up!

## Our assignment as the church is to control and patrol the heavenly places.

It is crucial that the church realizes our responsibility to govern in the heavenly places. As we get closer to the end of the age, demonic activity will increase. Therefore, the church has to exercise our authority over families, cities, states, and nations like never before. We must really become skilled in heavenly warfare. We must think spirit and spirit realm first. One of the frustrations I have continually is when I see believers trying to fix spiritual problems with earthly solutions. It will never happen. If the issue is spiritual, it is an exercise in futility to keep throwing natural solutions or reasoning at the problem. Instead of an exercise in futility, we need an exercise in authority. Only a member of the blood-washed church can do that.

Satan has tried to keep us ignorant of this authority. He knows that we have it, so he tries to keep us from knowing we have it. I'm reminded of the story in Acts 19:11-20. God was working mighty miracles through Paul, so that even handkerchiefs and aprons were brought from his body to the sick and they were healed. Some Jewish exorcists, the sons of Sceva, took it upon themselves to call the name of the Lord Jesus over those who had evil spirits, saying, *"We exorcise you by the Jesus whom Paul preaches."* This is the revelation I want you to receive. The demons answered, *"Jesus I know, and Paul I know; but who are you?"* It is very apparent to me from this statement that evil spirits know us and the authority we have. They did not recognize the authority of the sons of Sceva. In essence, they said, "We don't have to obey you because you have no authority over us." You see, the sons of Sceva thought that they could do what Paul did by saying what Paul said, only to find out that it's not what you speak but where you speak from that really matters. You must speak from a position of authority! You can say the name of Jesus, but unless you're in the name of Jesus, you don't have authority. The authority doesn't come from the church. It comes through the church from Christ. If you're not in Christ or part of the Lord's church, you are not authorized to speak on His behalf or in His authority. But if you are, then even the demons know it and are subject to you in His authority.

## You can say the name of Jesus, but unless you're in the name of Jesus, you don't have authority.

I'm reminded of a situation that happened several years ago at the church I used to pastor. While I was preaching, a man from off the street burst through the back door of the sanctuary. This was before we had sufficient training and security ministries in our church.

He came through the door screaming with a loud voice and came running down the middle aisle of the church. I had recently been preaching about spiritual warfare and several other things that dealt with who we are in Christ. So at the time this occurred, I was full of conviction and faith about our power to deal with demonic forces. As this man burst through the door and came down the aisle, I didn't know if he was armed or possessed or what the problem was. But as he ran toward me right in the middle of my sermon, out of my spirit I commanded him to stop and sit down, and then I kept right on preaching! I wish I could tell you how I did it, but the truth of the matter is that I said it before I knew it. It just came out as I was preaching. It was as if he hit a wall and dropped straight his knees and stayed there frozen for several minutes. The members were astonished, as was I, at the sight of this man sitting in the middle aisle unable to move. I was so surprised by what happened that I continued preaching for a few minutes with him sitting right there in the aisle. Of course, I eventually stopped preaching, and the ushers brought him forward and we ministered deliverance to him. That was the first time in my life and ministry that I saw a manifestation of supernatural authority over the enemy. It changed my life forever.

This authority that we have must be released as a weapon of mass destruction against the kingdom of darkness. In Matthew 16:18-19, Jesus gave the church its assignment. He declared that the mission of the church is to make sure that the gates of hell do not prevail against it! Once again, this reveals to us that our assignment is in the heavens first! We are established for the purpose of binding and loosing. I love how the Amplified Bible, Classic Edition explains Matthew 16:19. It states:

> *I will give you the keys of the kingdom of heaven; and whatever you bind (declare to be improper and unlawful) on earth must be what is already bound in heaven; and whatever you loose (declare lawful) on earth must be what is already loosed in heaven.*

It is clear our assignment is to allow what Heaven allows and to not allow what Heaven has not allowed. Simply put, our assignment is to not allow satan's assignments to manifest in the earth. That's why Jesus seated us in heavenly places far above them in rank and authority! It was to cut off their access and assignments in the earth. It is time that we sit down in the heavenly places as the rulers we were truly created to be. As you sit in this seat of authority, there is one thing I want to keep at the forefront of your mind. Remember, He raised us up together. Meaning, you don't have to work for this seat. You don't have to qualify for this seat. He seated you here when you became a part of the family. Ephesians 1:3 tells us that we are blessed with every spiritual blessing in heavenly places in Christ. There are natural blessings and there are spiritual blessings. You are blessed in both realms, and one of your spiritual blessings is authority. I want you to receive the blessing! It is a privilege to rule with Christ—a privilege that He died for you to have. It was His good pleasure to restore and extend the authority to you that Adam lost. You already have this authority, so you might as well use it. Sit down!

## It is a privilege to rule with Christ—a privilege that He died for you to have.

One thing I would like to emphasize about authority is that it doesn't require feeling to be exercised. Because we are spiritual and emotional beings, we often think we must feel powerful in order to be powerful. But authority is not felt. Ability is felt, but not authority. In Mark 5:25-34, you will find the story about the woman with the issue of blood. It is not my goal to teach about the whole story. I only want to highlight a certain part of it so that you can understand the difference between authority and ability. When Jesus was touched by the woman with the issue of blood, He asked, *"Who touched Me?"* because He felt virtue leave His body. When the woman made a demand on His power, the anointing was released and was felt by Him and her. Therefore, *dunamis,* the Greek word for *power* and *ability,* can be felt when it is released. But it is not so with authority. *Exousia,* which is the Greek word for *authority,* means "rights and permission granted to rule and authority."

# When you speak, all the authority of Heaven is ready to back you up!

Too many believers do not know they have authority. They are waiting to feel powerful. But authority is not given or released that way. Authority is a right and rule given by position. It is invested. When Jesus declared that you are seated far above principalities and powers, the seat itself has invested you with authority no matter how you feel. If you are in Christ, you have authority. Because of this fact, to enforce this authority is a decision. You don't have to feel it, but you do have to believe it. You do not need to fast for authority. You do not need to pray for authority. You do not have to worship or praise for authority. All you must be is born for authority—or, better yet, born again—and you have it. When circumstances and the enemy try to dominate your life, you must stand in the middle of the situation and take authority over it, whether you feel like it or not. You do not need your emotions to agree with you. Angels and demons are not waiting for an emotional response from you; they are waiting for a command. When you speak, all the authority of Heaven is ready to back you up!

I want to reiterate to you that there are certain things that you have been born with! You did not earn them or work for them. You were simply born with an inheritance of authority. You were placed in that seat. Now, you are in it through Christ—you must decide to sit in it and stay in it. If someone left you an inheritance of a billion dollars in their will and it was in an account in their name and the bank called you to come and claim it, would you tell the bank that you would have to fast and pray before you come get it? Of course you wouldn't. You would be in the car with tires screeching to get there to claim it. Jesus is saying to all of us, "I have left you an inheritance. It is in My will and in My name, and I need you to come claim it. You don't have to earn it. I left it for you. And it would give Me so much pleasure to see you have it."

I know so much is happening around us, and even to us, that sometimes we think that we are supposed to win some and lose some. I'm here to tell you that is not God's will for us. We are to never be defeated by the enemy. I realize we are not perfected humans in our development or in our spiritual maturity. This is why I'm writing this book—so that we can get the faith to live in what we have and stop allowing satan to steal it. Things happen in our lives for various reasons. Sometimes we break spiritual laws. Other times we violate natural laws. Other times we are faced with the curses in the earth or human error. Then there is plain old demonic attack. No matter how the situation arises, once you find yourself in it, start taking authority to change it! Satan is going to test you over your seat. He hates you for your position over him. However, you must hate him even more for daring to violate God's word concerning you. He knows that you and I are off-limits to him as the offspring God, but he doesn't care. So you must arise, or better yet stay seated, and put him under your feet. It requires nothing more than for you to simply believe it!

It is amazing to consider that as I sit in my office typing this book in the natural, my spirit is recognized in another realm by angels and demons as a son of God. What I must look like to them. If only we could see ourselves beyond the natural, we could change the world. In this earth we make such a huge deal about race and ethnicity. We even spend money to trace our roots and ancestry to discover all the intricate strands of nationalities that make up who we are. Let me be very clear, I am not saying that it is wrong or vain to trace your roots. And neither is it insignificant to know your natural heritage. You should be very proud of your race, nationality, and culture. However, knowing those things do not bring any victory or empowerment in the realm of the spirit. I tell people all of the time, while I'm proud to be born black because that is the nationality that the Lord chose for me in order to fulfill His purpose for my life in the earth, that is not the most important thing to me. I am much prouder to be born again! Because being born black or white, Hispanic or Asian, or whatever nationality, does not come with a covenant, anointing, or authority. Being born again does! And it is that identity that gives you victory over the enemy.

There is nothing in the natural that gives you pre-eminence over the adversary—only what you are in the spirit. It doesn't matter if you feel you are not intelligent, articulate, or gifted in the natural; you still are the highest-ranking being in the spiritual realm if you are a child of God. You don't have to be an apostle, prophet, evangelist, pastor, or teacher to have this ascended position of authority. The enemy is terrified at the knowledge of this, because the primary way he defeats us is by making us feel inferior within ourselves. But it has nothing to do with you or anything about you! You are superior to him because of who you are in Christ—period!

# CHAPTER 6

# AUTHORITY AND WORDS

It is just as important to teach on the ascension as it is the resurrection. This ascended position that we have in Christ is where our occupation and assignment are. That is why in this chapter we will take a further look at the assignment and responsibility that has been given to the church in this aspect of binding and loosing. As I stated earlier, the Amplified Bible is very clear in Matthew 16:19 that the phrase "binding and loosing" means to "allow and not allow"! Now that we know the mission, the question is, how do we do it? And the answer is with your mouth. That's why a revelation of authority is so vital. It is because authority is released with words. Words are how we govern the realm of the spirit.

We can see this clearly in Genesis 1:3. As God looked over the earth, which was without form and void and with the darkness over the face of the deep, the Bible declares that God said, *"Let there be light."* It's amazing to comprehend that God fixed the whole earth and its disorderly condition with words. He did not move His hand; He simply opened His mouth, and the authority of His words brought order to the earth realm. The Bible tells us in John 4:24, *"God is Spirit,"* meaning that God exists in a realm that is not seen. But just because the spirit realm is unseen does not mean it is unreal. As a matter of fact, it is more real than the natural realm, because the natural realm had to respond to the spirit realm.

This reveals to us that heavenly things have authority over earthly things. It also tells us that heavenly commands are how we change earthly situations. This is vital because this is how the keys of the Kingdom work. We simply take the authority given to us by the Father, and we allow or disallow in the earth what He desires. The power to bring change in the earth realm is in the hands of the church. The assignment given to the church is to hover over the earth, being seated in heavenly places, and then speak the word of God to bring order to the chaos in the earth. Wow! What a responsibility. When the church understands this, we will inflict massive damage and destruction to the kingdom of darkness. When Jesus declared, *"On this rock I will build My church"* (Matthew 16:18), He was not referring to an institution or a religious organization; He was referring to a governing body that sits in the heavens and legislates His will on earth.

# The power to bring change in the earth realm is in the hands of the church.

Again, this legislative authority given back to humanity is a restoration of the original method and mandate given to Adam. I never will forget sitting in a service at a minister's conference when one of the speakers mentioned Genesis 2:8 and the original Hebrew meaning in the phrase when man became a "living soul." She said that instead of man just becoming a living soul, he also actually became a "speaking spirit"! Something leaped in my spirit in that moment. I knew I had just heard a master key to the revelation of the Kingdom.

When God made man, He made him a spirit. Then He put the spirit in a body. Then He gave the spirit the authority to speak. Not only is the spirit man given the authority to speak, but Adam was given the authority to speak on behalf of God and Heaven in the earth. This is how he would exercise his dominion of the earth and everything God created. The authority was granted to the spirit man! As Adam spoke as a sprit being, everything in that realm had to obey him also. Therefore, through the body he had authority in the earth, and through the spirit he had authority in the spirit realm. God made him a speaking spirit so that he could rule the physical earth despite being a spiritual being. The way that Adam did that was with speaking!

God intended that spirits with bodies would be in authority in the earth. That's why when a spirit speaks in the earth realm things begin to shift. Satan knows this. This is one of the main reasons satan wanted to entice Adam to sin. It was so that he would be stripped of this authority to speak on behalf of Heaven in the realm of the spirit and over the earth. This is one of the most significant things that Jesus restored with the resurrection. When He declared all authority in Heaven and earth was given to Him, He was declaring that a resurrected spirit man had regained the authority in the realm of the spirit and on earth. As God authorized Adam to speak on His behalf in Genesis 1, now Jesus can authorize the church to speak on His behalf in the new covenant. This was the main purpose of the new birth! It was to restore your spirit to its original condition so that you could be authorized to speak again on behalf of Heaven and over the earth. It was God's authority given to Adam. Now, it's Jesus' authority given to you. We need to see ourselves as not just human beings, but also as speaking spirits who effect change in the earth realm when we speak.

This understanding of words and authority caused Jesus to marvel at the centurion in Matthew 8:5-13:

> *Now when Jesus had entered Capernaum, a centurion came to Him, pleading with Him, saying, "Lord, my servant is lying at home paralyzed, dreadfully tormented."*
> *And Jesus said to him, "I will come and heal him."*
> *The centurion answered and said, "Lord, I am not worthy that You should come under my roof. But only speak a word, and my servant will be healed. For I also am a man under authority, having soldiers under me.*

*And I say to this one, 'Go,' and he goes; and
to another, 'Come,' and he comes; and to my
servant, 'Do this,' and he does it."*

*When Jesus heard it, He marveled, and said
to those who followed, "Assuredly, I say to
you, I have not found such great faith, not
even in Israel! And I say to you that many will
come from east and west, and sit down with
Abraham, Isaac, and Jacob in the kingdom
of heaven. But the sons of the kingdom will
be cast out into outer darkness. There will be
weeping and gnashing of teeth." Then Jesus
said to the centurion, "Go your way; and as
you have believed, so let it be done for you."
And his servant was healed that same hour.*

Jesus said that a revelation of authority is what gave
this man great faith. The thing that made Jesus marvel
at this centurion was that he understood authority. He
recognized that when you are in authority, you do not
have to be present physically because the authority is
released in words. When you are in authority, you do not
have to be present for your words to be obeyed. If you
are in authority over what you are speaking to, what you
are speaking to must submit. And what this centurion
realized was that Jesus had authority over his servant's
condition. It's amazing to realize that the centurion
caught what everyone else had missed. He understood
that Jesus was doing what He did by authority.

There are so many things about the Word of God that we will never have great faith in until we understand authority. Authority is one of the keys to the Kingdom. It is my sincere belief that this passage is one of the most important passages in all of scripture. Remember, this made Jesus marvel! Not only did the centurion have a revelation of Jesus' authority, he also had a revelation of how it is released. Being a man under authority, he understood that when he spoke, the authority he held would enforce his words. My question to the church is, "Have we truly realized who we are under?"

As members of the body of Christ, Ephesians 1:22-23 tells us that when Jesus arose from the dead, God *"put all things under His feet, and gave Him to be head over all things to the church, which is His body, the fullness of Him who fills all in all."* This tells us who we are under! Christ is the head over the church. He also happens to be the head over all things! That means there is nothing in Heaven or earth that is not underneath His authority. When we speak as His body, we are speaking under His authority.

I was preaching in a conference in Hampton, Virginia. The Lord had been dealing with me about authority and healing the sick, like this centurion experienced. He said to me, "When you pray for the sick tonight, don't pray for Me to heal them, and don't pray about their situation. Instead, I want you to speak to the disease or ailment in My name and release My authority. Don't pray about it, but instead talk to it and release My authority."

## There is nothing in Heaven or earth that is not underneath Jesus' authority. When we speak as His body, we are speaking under His authority.

That night as people came to the altar, a young lady walked up with her elderly mother. She informed me that her mother was totally blind. I pulled them both up to the front of the altar and told them what I was going to do and say. Under a tremendous anointing, I shouted, "In the name of Jesus, I speak to your eyes and command them to be open!" Then I removed my hands from covering her eyes and said, "Tell me what you see!"

She started crying and said, "I see you!" God instantly opened her eyes in front of the congregation. Her daughter started weeping and praising God at the sight of her mother's miracle. I started shouting and praising God as well as the whole church. After that night, I got the revelation of what Peter did at the Gate Beautiful in Acts 3:6 when he said, *"Silver and gold I do not have, but what I do have I give you: In the name of Jesus Christ of Nazareth, rise up and walk."* Peter said, "I don't have any money to give you, but what I do have is authority!" And he released it with his mouth, and this man was made whole.

After that experience in Virginia, the Lord revealed to me that if I would release the authority, He would release the ability! Authority plus power is the formula for the miraculous! And that authority is released when you speak. That is why the scripture tells us in Colossians 3:17, *"And whatever you do in word or deed, do all in the name of the Lord Jesus, giving thanks to God the Father through Him."* As members of the body of Christ, we speak and function underneath His authority. Therefore, we must be very careful to watch our words. The highest use of our words is not just for conversation, but for legislation!

Because we are to govern the earth with our words, it is very critical that we say what Jesus said. Often when we see situations out of order in the earth or experience attacks of the enemy, we talk about the situation. But if anything is going to change, we must talk to the situation and bring the authority of Heaven on the scene. It is now that the church must rethink and redefine our purpose and assignment in the earth. We are here for the purpose of ruling and stewarding the earth realm on behalf of King Jesus. Singing, shouting, dancing, and going to church are all good, but in addition to that we must begin to deal with the kingdom of darkness. Jesus meant it when He said in John 14:12-14:

> *Most assuredly, I say to you, he who believes*
> *in Me, the works that I do he will do also; and*
> *greater works than these he will do, because*
> *I go to My Father. And whatever you ask in*
> *My name, that I will do, that the Father may*
> *be glorified in the Son. If you ask anything in*
> *My name, I will do it.*

What a word and revelation. Jesus is saying, "When I go to the Father, I am going to bring you into a position with the Father that I occupy. When you get in that position, you will be able to use the same authority that I have. Then, whatever you ask the Father, if it is under My authority (in My name), the Father will grant it to you."

It is my humble belief that for us to be truly effective in prayer, we must understand authority. One of the major purposes of prayer is to get the mind of God about a matter in the earth, and then release the authority of Heaven to address it. Prayer is about releasing authority! Prayer is not designed to have a little talk with Jesus and tell Him all about your troubles. It is designed to have a little talk with Jesus and then tell your troubles about Him and what He said! I think it is now clear what Solomon was trying to tell us in Proverbs 18:21 when he said, *"Death and life are in the power of the tongue, and those who love it will eat its fruit."* There is so much authority released in words that Solomon said you will eventually experience what your words have materialized.

In that phrase "power of the tongue," the Hebrew word for *power* is *yad,* which means "hand, strength, or power." I believe that one of the things Solomon was trying to tell us is that our words act like a hand in the spirit realm and in the earth! Our words possess like our hands. Sometimes, to change situations, you don't have to use your physical hands; you just need to open your mouth and your words will move things just like your hands would! That's what the centurion did! In essence, he said, "You don't have to come lay Your physical hands on my servant; open Your mouth, and Your words are just as powerful as Your hands." Now that's some power! It is time that we who are members of the church weaponize our words and release them like arrows out of our mouths to bring Heaven's authority on the scene in every situation.

# CHAPTER 7

# RULING THE HEAVENLIES

This has always and will forever be a spiritual battle! When lucifer fell from Heaven, the Bible declares in Revelation 12:9 that he was cast down to the earth. He was banished from Heaven and only allowed to exist under Heaven and function over the earth. Therefore, he is very active in the earth realm. There is something crucial at this point that we need to understand or remember. Satan is a spirit! He is not a man. He and his minions are evil spirits. Why is this of utmost importance to remember? It is because when satan fell, even though he is a spirit, his fall affected the physical realm. All the chaos on earth was brought about by spirits operating in the earth realm.

As I revealed earlier in Chapter 1, after God restored the earth, He said in Genesis 1:26, *"Let Us make man."* Why? Because of lucifer! If lucifer had not fallen, humanity wouldn't have ever been created. We were not created to just interact with one another as humans; we were created to interact with fallen spirits, angels and demons, and even the Holy Spirit for that matter. When we understand this spiritual dimension, it will bring greater clarity to why God made humanity like He did. God is a Spirit! Hebrews 12:9 says that He is the Father of spirits, which tells us that God creates spirits. Therefore, He rules spirits. That's why He is the master of the spirit realm.

Another reason why humankind was created spirit, soul, and body is because part of humankind's existence and function happens in another realm. It is the spirit part of you that registers in the spirit realm. You are seen, felt, and heard in that realm. And since it is the realm where you exist, it is also the realm where your authority exists and is exercised. Remember when I was talking about Paul and the sons of Sceva in Chapter 4? Do you remember what the demons said to the sons after they tried to cast them out? *"Jesus, I know. Paul, I know. But who are you?"* It is because you are seen and heard in that realm. If you are a child of the King, they know it!

I bring this up because we are preoccupied with the natural realm. Don't get me wrong—we must live and function in the natural realm. However, we must not forget that we also live in another realm! It is the realm of the spirit that we have been called to police! It is the realm of the spirit that we have been called to dominate. And if we would diligently police the realm of the spirit, we wouldn't need as many policemen to police the realm of the natural! The earth is in the shape that it is in because of the failure of the church to take its place in the spirit realm.

As we turn our focus on the spirit realm, we will begin to see amazing things happen in the natural realm. This is the heart's desire of Jesus and the Father revealed in the model prayer in Matthew 6:10: *"Your kingdom come. Your will be done on earth as it is in heaven."* For that prayer to be fulfilled, the church must take its place in the heavenlies, and do it now. This battle over earth is about spiritual supremacy. Which spirits will rule? God made humankind spirits so that we could rule the spirit realm. Then he put us in bodies so that we could steward and rule the natural realm on earth. The attitude that we must have while walking around in the earth is that of a landlord over the earth.

When I say "over the earth," I'm picturing it like an umbrella. We must become militant about our assignment to cover the earth from the wickedness of satan and his assignments. This is what we call war in the heavenlies. It is about meeting the battle in the heavens before it can manifest in the earth. Ephesians 6:11 warns us that we are wrestling against the "wiles" of the devil. That word means "schemes." There is constant scheming going on all the time in the realm of the spirit. Sadly, most of the time we don't know what was schemed until it manifests. By then, we are playing defense and dealing with the fallout of demonic attacks. It is God's will for us to know the plans of the enemy before they manifest. For that to happen, we must become spiritually vigilant. This is one of the main reasons the Holy Spirit was given to us—so that He could reveal to us the things of the Spirit in the spirit. We must take our responsibility in the jurisdiction we have been given authority over more seriously. If we do that, we can stop some of the schemes of the enemy from ever coming to fruition. So let's be more committed to shut him down!

Satan and his schemes should not be our only emphasis in the spirit realm. There is also another force operating in this realm—the angelic hosts of Heaven who serve God. I don't think the body of Christ has talked about angels enough. Angels are a topic that we need to constantly preach and talk about! I cannot stress enough the importance of angels. The spirit realm is filled with these mighty warriors just waiting to carry out the will of the Father in the earth. To do so, they need the church to give them His commands and release them. In Hebrews 1:13-14, the Bible is very clear that the angels have been sent to minister for us—those who are the heirs of salvation. They are still working for God through us, just like they did in the Old and New Testament. They are mighty weapons in the spirit realm, and they hearken to our voice as the church. Much of what happens in the earth is dependent upon our employment of them.

Now, I'm about to say something that is really shocking! If this is a battle in which the spirit realm will rule the earth and we as the church have authority in the realm of the spirit and have the angels at our command, why are we not winning every battle? In 2 Kings 6:8-18, we have an incredible story and explanation about the spirit realm:

> *Now the king of Syria was making war against Israel; and he consulted with his servants, saying, "My camp will be in such and such a place." And the man of God sent to the king of Israel, saying, "Beware that you*

*do not pass this place, for the Syrians are coming down there." Then the king of Israel sent someone to the place of which the man of God had told him. Thus he warned him, and he was watchful there, not just once or twice.*

*Therefore the heart of the king of Syria was greatly troubled by this thing; and he called his servants and said to them, "Will you not show me which of us is for the king of Israel?"*

*And one of his servants said, "None, my lord, O king; but Elisha, the prophet who is in Israel, tells the king of Israel the words that you speak in your bedroom."*

*So he said, "Go and see where he is, that I may send and get him."*

*And it was told him, saying, "Surely he is in Dothan."*

*Therefore he sent horses and chariots and a great army there, and they came by night and surrounded the city. And when the servant of the man of God arose early and went out, there was an army, surrounding the city with horses and chariots. And his servant said to him, "Alas, my master! What shall we do?"*

*So he answered, "Do not fear, for those who are with us are more than those who are with them." And Elisha prayed, and said, "Lord, I pray, open his eyes that he may see." Then the Lord opened the eyes of the young man, and he saw. And behold, the mountain was full of horses and chariots of fire all around Elisha. So when the Syrians came down to him, Elisha prayed to the Lord, and said, "Strike this people, I pray, with blindness." And He struck them with blindness according to the word of Elisha.*

Wow! There are so many revelations in the passage. The phrase that leaped off the page to me was this statement, in verse 16, when Elisha said, *"Do not fear, for those who are with us are more than those who are with them."* In the spirit realm you are never outnumbered! If only our eyes were opened to see the power and activity we control in the spirit realm. We could shake nations! There are always more with you! That's why I get frustrated when I hear people talking more about the devil and what he's doing than they talk about God and what He's doing! If Elisha, a prophet in the Old Covenant, understood this, how much more should the heirs of salvation and the mighty ekklesia of Heaven understand this!

It is high time that we discern what the enemy is scheming for our lives, families, and nations and release the mighty hosts of Heaven to spoil his plans! Not only are those with us more than those against us, but those with us are also greater and stronger than those against us. The Word declares in Psalm 103:20, *"Bless the Lord, you His angels, who excel in strength, who do His word, heeding the voice of His word."* They excel to whatever strength is needed to fulfill God's word. They are more powerful than demons!

---

# It is high time that we discern what the enemy is scheming for our lives, families, and nations and release the mighty hosts of Heaven to spoil his plans!

---

I could spend hours talking about the scriptures that highlight angelic strength and power, but instead I would like to give you a personal testimony of something that happened one night while at church several years ago. We had been praying for a young lady to be delivered from demonic possession. The situation was so intense at the altar that I dismissed the service and only allowed the musicians and the elders to remain after the service. As I began to pray for her, she began to manifest unusual strength and a voice began to speak out of her and say, "You can't cast me out, I'm going to kill her."

As we all stood there determined to get her delivered, I reached out to touch her. When I did, the demon began telling me to get my hands off her. As I continued to pray, she grabbed my arms and began digging her fingernails into my skin. As her nails clawed into my arms, the elders started to grab her and pull her off me. Then, for some reason, I said, "Don't do it." Instead, I shouted, "Angels of the Lord, make this spirit get its hands off me!" I don't know what made me do it this way, except for the Spirit of God. Suddenly, it was as if someone unlocked her fingers and pulled her arms back as if she was under arrest. As she snarled at me in defiance, I shouted, "You better not touch me again," and the spirit obeyed. After several more minutes, glory to God, she was set free that night as we all watched in amazement.

I share this story because that night changed my life and ministry forever. I knew for a fact that the angelic hosts of Heaven were real and that they were mightier than demons. Since then, I have seen so many displays of angels excelling in strength to stop the kingdom of darkness in its tracks. If we as the church would stand in our authority and release these mighty angels, they are willing and more than able to get the job done! It is this awareness and confidence in the realm of spiritual activity that delivers us from fear. These angelic beings are so capable and responsible to deliver you. Psalm 91:11 is a favorite passage of many believers. It declares, *"He shall give His angels charge over you, to keep you in all of your ways."* God has commanded them to keep you! So you know that they are going to follow through with the Lord's command. They will keep the charge, but we must keep the faith that they will work on our behalf.

I have often been baffled over the years at how the church has preached the devil so big and the Spirit of God so small. We are constantly talking about what the enemy is doing and how he is attacking and how we must be on the lookout for him. While I agree that satan is busy and that we must be sober and vigilant to his activity, I also believe the Holy Spirit is busy and moving to destroy the works of the enemy.

> *How God anointed Jesus of Nazareth with the Holy Spirit and with power, who went about doing good and healing all who were oppressed by the devil, for God was with Him* (Acts 10:38).

This is what we should have been shouting from the rooftops. The Holy Spirit is the greatest power in the earth! Satan and all the evil spirits ever created must bow to His presence and in His presence! And where does the Spirit abide? You guessed it—in you and me if you're born again! You are not alone. You and I have the third person of the Godhead with us. Acts 1:8 said that you and I would receive power after the Holy Ghost came on us. That power is in the spirit. It is released from a spiritual being, in a spiritual realm, and it brings to a screeching halt all the spiritual activity of the enemy. Simply put, when the Spirit moves, all other spiritual activity stops moving!

# When the Spirit moves, all other spiritual activity stops moving!

Here is something that must be revealed and discussed about the Holy Spirit. He will not override your authority! You must exercise your authority in order to see His mighty ability! The Spirit works with and through the mighty name of Jesus.

> *And these signs will follow those who believe: In My name they will cast out demons; they will speak with new tongues; they will take up serpents; and if they drink anything deadly, it will by no means hurt them; they will lay hands on the sick, and they will recover* (Mark 16:17-18).

The scripture is clear that this will happen in His name or authority. If we release His authority, these signs will follow because His ability follows His authority. Authority plus ability equals supernatural power! Think of it like this, a police officer has a badge and a gun! One backs up the other. One represents authority and the other represents the ability to carry out the authority! Jesus gave the church His authority, but He did not give the church His ability. That belongs only to the Holy Ghost. But the Holy Ghost has been given to the church to release whatever ability is required to back up the church's authority.

## God's ability follows His authority. Authority plus ability equals supernatural power!

I want you to be more aware of heavenly or spirit-realm activity. Scripture is very clear that the assignment to control spiritual activity in the heavenly places has been given to the church. Decide today that you will rule the atmosphere over your life from this day forward.

# CHAPTER 8

# HOLD THE LINE

At the time I'm writing this book, the world has just experienced a global pandemic. There is also war being waged by a global superpower upon a neighboring country. It seems as if things are intensifying in the heavenly realm and spilling over into the earth realm. I want to be clear—not every negative event that happens in the earth realm is caused by demonic activity. Some events are caused by human decision and error. The Bible declares that the carnal mind is enmity against God. Some of the things that transpire on earth are the consequences of human choices. But what many people don't realize is that a lot of human decision is being influenced by spiritual activity.

It is vitally important to realize that we will not be able to stop all demonic schemes from manifesting in the earth realm. Satan will always have a kingdom here and he will always have a people in the earth to work through. But the church has been given immense authority to control much of it. One revelation I believe is key to the church understanding its authority is an understanding of the church age. What is the church age? The church age is a period of time revealed in Daniel 9:20-27:

> *Now while I was speaking, praying, and con-*
> *fessing my sin and the sin of my people Israel,*
> *and presenting my supplication before the*
> *Lord my God for the holy mountain of my*
> *God, yes, while I was speaking in prayer, the*

*man Gabriel, whom I had seen in the vision at the beginning, being caused to fly swiftly, reached me about the time of the evening offering. And he informed me, and talked with me, and said, "O Daniel, I have now come forth to give you skill to understand. At the beginning of your supplications the command went out, and I have come to tell you, for you are greatly beloved; therefore consider the matter, and understand the vision:*

*"Seventy weeks are determined for your people and for your holy city, to finish the transgression, to make an end of sins, to make reconciliation for iniquity, to bring in everlasting righteousness, to seal up vision and prophecy, and to anoint the Most Holy.*

*"Know therefore and understand, that from the going forth of the command to restore and build Jerusalem until Messiah the Prince, there shall be seven weeks and sixty-two weeks; the street shall be built again, and the wall, even in troublesome times.*

*"And after the sixty-two weeks Messiah shall be cut off, but not for Himself; and the people of the prince who is to come shall destroy the city and the sanctuary. The end of it shall be with a flood, and till the end of the war desolations are determined. Then he shall confirm a covenant with many for one week; but in*

*the middle of the week He shall bring an end to sacrifice and offering. And on the wing of abominations shall be one who makes desolate, even until the consummation, which is determined, is poured out on the desolate."*

Daniel is prophetically declaring a period that stretches from the restoration of the temple in Israel all the way to the second coming of the Lord Jesus Christ to the earth. My desire is not to look into this chapter with an end-time point of view. Neither do I want you to focus on the second coming. Those things are of great importance, and I do not want to minimize them. What I want to give you is enough insight so that you can decode this vision as it relates to the authority that has been given to the church in this age. Daniel is describing what will happen in a time period of 70 weeks. These 70 weeks are not literal weeks but, prophetically, 70 weeks of years! In this prophecy, a week is a seven-year period. What he saw was that God would take seventy seven-year periods and manifest the things that the angel shared with Daniel during that time.

Of those 70 weeks, 69 have been fulfilled. Daniel said that in seven weeks they would restore and build Jerusalem, and 49 years from the day Daniel spoke that, Jerusalem was rebuilt. Daniel also said that in 62 weeks the Messiah would appear and be cut off, and exactly 434 years from the moment Daniel spoke that, Jesus' ministry began and ended. This so important to know because there is one more week that has yet to be fulfilled. It is the last seven-year period known as the tribulation. That is the period in which the antichrist shall arise and be destroy after a seven-year period. He will be destroyed by the glorious advent of Jesus' Second Coming to the earth.

The question is, "What is taking so long for the last seven years of Daniel's prophecy to be revealed?" The answer? The glorious church! That's right! There was a gap between week 69 and 70 of Daniel's prophecy that was not revealed to him. As a matter of fact, the Bible declares it wasn't revealed to anyone except the Godhead. As I stated earlier, the church was a mystery hidden in God. The church age is a period between Daniel's week 69 and 70 that manifests the Kingdom of Heaven on earth until the catching away of the church. The purpose of this age is to minister the redemptive grace and work of Christ to all people and manifest the victory that was wrought in Christ over satan and his kingdom through the cross. The mandate to the church age is given by Jesus in Matthew 28:18-20:

> *And Jesus came and spoke to them, saying, "All authority has been given to Me in heaven and on earth. Go therefore and make disciples of all the nations, baptizing them in the name of the Father and of the Son and of the Holy Spirit, teaching them to observe all things that I have commanded you; and lo, I am with you always, even to the end of the age." Amen.*

**The purpose of this age is to minister the redemptive grace and work of Christ to all people and manifest the victory that was wrought in Christ over satan and his kingdom through the cross.**

Now couple this with what Jesus said in Mark 16:15-18 when He stated:

> *And He said to them, "Go into all the world and preach the gospel to every creature. He who believes and is baptized will be saved; but he who does not believe will be condemned. And these signs will follow those who believe: In My name they will cast out demons; they will speak with new tongues; they will take up serpents; and if they drink anything deadly, it will by no means hurt them; they will lay hands on the sick, and they will recover."*

It is very clear that the assignment for the church age brings a display of power and authority through the church that the earth has not experienced. No one throughout the ages could foresee that the resurrection of Jesus would authorize and deputize an entire age of believers to go throughout the earth destroying the works and plans of the devil. Therefore, the revelation of the church age is so key. In the church age, the church holds the authority! We have the right to resist the kingdom of darkness in this age.

After the catching away of the church, a phrase that some call the Rapture, there will be no force on earth to resist the kingdom of darkness. The church is so powerful that the Word of God declares that the antichrist can't even come on the scene until the church has been removed. The thing that will make the tribulation so horrible is that there will be no governing force here to resist it. Sure, the Holy Spirit will still be here, and many will still come to the saving knowledge of Jesus Christ, but it will come at a very high price and cost many their lives. In the church age, there is supposed to be a level of dominion exercised over the enemy by the church. We must become more determined than ever to not let the devil run our age. Second Thessalonians 2:1-12 explains what the antichrist will try to accomplish, and what satan is trying to accomplish even before the antichrist is manifested.

*Now, brethren, concerning the coming of our Lord Jesus Christ and our gathering together to Him, we ask you, not to be soon shaken in mind or troubled, either by spirit or by word or by letter, as if from us, as though the day of Christ had come. Let no one deceive you by any means; for that Day will not come unless the falling away comes first, and the man of sin is revealed, the son of perdition, who opposes and exalts himself above all that is called God or that is worshiped, so that he sits as God in the temple of God, showing himself that he is God.*

*Do you not remember that when I was still with you I told you these things? And now you know what is restraining, that he may be revealed in his own time. For the mystery of lawlessness is already at work; only He who now restrains will do so until He is taken out of the way. And then the lawless one will be revealed, whom the Lord will consume with the breath of His mouth and destroy with the brightness of His coming. The coming of the lawless one is according to the working of Satan, with all power, signs, and lying wonders, and with all unrighteous deception among those who perish, because they did not receive the love of the truth, that they might be saved. And for this reason God will send them strong delusion, that they should believe the lie, that they all may be condemned who*

> *did not believe the truth but had pleasure in*
> *unrighteousness.*

The key phrase to me is found in verse 7. The mystery of lawlessness is already at work! The antichrist is not even coming into existence until we are gone. But his spirit is already at work in the earth. That's what we are resisting. We are the restrainers verse 7 is talking about. The spirit of God working through the church in this age is supposed to be the restraining force! As long as we are still in this age, which will not end until the catching away of the church, we must hold the line. We must take ownership of the age and rule it like we are in charge.

Satan knows that the church has the power to resist him. James 4:7 says, *"Therefore submit to God. Resist the devil and he will flee from you."* The word for *flee* is the Greek word *pheugo*. It means "to run away, shun, avoid, or escape." In this age, no believer should ever be afraid or have trepidation about the devil. He should be afraid of us! And he is. Satan and the evil spirits know that if you exercise your authority, they have no choice but to flee. Why? Because they know what happened the last time they ran up against God's authority! In Luke 10:17-20, Jesus sent the 70 disciples out to minister instead of Him. But before He sent them out, He gave them His power and authority to minister with. This is what the scripture recorded upon their return:

> *Then the seventy returned with joy, saying,*
> *"Lord, even the demons are subject to us*
> *in Your name." And He said to them, "I*

*saw Satan fall like lightning from heaven. Behold, I give you the authority to trample on serpents and scorpions, and over all the power of the enemy, and nothing shall by any means hurt you. Nevertheless do not rejoice in this, that the spirits are subject to you, but rather rejoice because your names are written in heaven."*

That means in the blink of an eye, satan was cast out! That's fast! I think sometimes we have the assumption that satan is somehow God's nemesis. But God has no rival! He has all authority. The Bible calls satan our adversary. That's why we must stand our ground in the authority granted to us in Christ and bring him under subjection. Just like the 70, we will come back rejoicing in victory and triumph every time.

As we look a little deeper into this age, one thing I would like to highlight is 2 Thessalonians 2:7, which declares *"the mystery of lawlessness is already at work."* What is the actual lawlessness that the enemy is trying to bring in, and how can we define it more clearly? This lawlessness is in two forms. On one hand it is to create a breach of law, and on the other hand it is to usher in a removal of law.

We are seeing things never before seen in the earth as I write this book. There is such unprecedented law-breaking going on throughout the nations of the world through crime and violence and wickedness. But one of the most shocking things that is happening is the removal of law on unprecedented levels as well. When I say removal of law, I mean the disregard for absolutes and moral statues instituted by God and His Word. The reason we see these laws being removed is because of the spirit of lawlessness that is at work in our age. These so-called new progressive ideologies are the work of the spirit of iniquity. The removal and redefining of what is right and wrong, male and female, clean and unclean is a result of satan wanting to produce a boundaryless society in the earth. The goal is to create the culture of hell on earth.

# We must flip the paradigm in this generation if we are going to see the Kingdom come in power in this age.

We are actually getting glimpses of what the tribulation period will look like when there are no laws or boundaries given or respected among people. The only thing resisting this agenda is the church. My fear is that the church is failing to really understand this battle. While we are focusing on natural laws and political maneuvering, the enemy is going mostly unresisted in the heavens where the real battle is—not just because the church is negligent, but because most of the church is unaware of it. These assignments must be cancelled in the spirit through prayers and decrees!

Don't get me wrong, there is and has always been a remnant that has understood this and engaged the enemy in the high places in this age. However, while the church is working through a remnant, satan is working through a majority. We must flip this paradigm in this generation if we are going to see the Kingdom come in power in this age. I highlighted Daniel's prophecy in this chapter because I want to emphasize our role in this age. We can shut down a lot of what of we are seeing in the earth realm. But it will take an army of saints and intercessors to stand in our authority and steward this age. Let's rise up and defend our ground. This is our time!

# CHAPTER 9

# A Time for War

The authority that God gave to Christ after the resurrection is now so expanded that it encompasses everything created except human will. I want to repeat that! The only thing that Christ and the church don't have authority over is people. Therefore, satan and evil spirits seek people to work through. It is because spirits hide behind human wills! This is a powerful revelation. They do this to shield themselves from authority. They understand that we as the church have authority over them, but they also understand that we don't have authority over people. So they influence people to do their bidding, thereby hiding themselves from having to directly deal with our authority.

Demon spirits know that I ultimately can't use my authority in another person's life without their consent. In other words, it's hard to cast out what someone else is letting in. Even in the example I gave earlier in Chapter 6 about the deliverance of the young lady, I had to get her to renounce some things first before she could be set free. Not every time is this necessary. Sometimes people have never consented to satan by choice in the first place. They are simply being deceived or seduced into a situation. Once you pray for them or intercede, the spirits are dealt with. But when people begin to yield to certain ideologies and behavior and reject the truth, it becomes very difficult to see breakthrough in their lives or circumstances.

It's so hard to remove certain principalities and powers from ruling over certain families, cities, states, and nations because the evil spirits have so influenced and engrained themselves in the thinking, behavior, and culture of the people that the people themselves don't even realize they are under satanic influence. It becomes a way of life, and the assignment of the church is to set them free! But to do this we must declare war. We must become very intentional about pulling down these strongholds. Second Corinthians 10:3-6 describes the war we are in. It says:

> For though we walk in the flesh, we do not war according to the flesh. For the weapons of our warfare are not carnal but mighty in God for pulling down strongholds, casting down arguments and every high thing that exalts itself against the knowledge of God, bringing every thought into captivity to the obedience of Christ, and being ready to punish all disobedience when your obedience is fulfilled.

Paul warns us that spiritual wars must be fought in the spirit realm. We are not dealing with just flesh and blood, but we are combatting spiritual reasoning and arguments that exalt themselves over the knowledge of God. Whenever you are dealing with a constant bombardment of thoughts, ideas, feelings, and ideologies that are against the knowledge of God's Word, you're dealing with demonic activity.

As I look back over my 30-plus years in ministry and my 50-plus years on earth, I have to say I have seen the kingdom of darkness take much ground in the church and the earth during my lifetime. I never would have imagined that we would be living in a world so twisted and wicked. Even within the church, the things being ordained and accepted are simply hard to believe. It would not be possible for satan to take this much ground in the earth unless he had taken it first in the spirit realm.

What you see is the result of spiritual wars fought over the territory. One thing has become very clear. Satan has declared all-out war on our families, children, cities, nations, and every institution and sphere on planet earth. The nations and the whole earth are shaking and trembling under the assault of the kingdom of darkness. We are being surrounded on every side, and it seems as if the walls are closing in. But at the same time, I can sense a remnant beginning to arise and form in the earth that the kingdom of darkness has never had to deal with. We are finally starting to realize our real identity, authority, and inheritance in Christ.

Every war that we fight in the spirit cannot be about what the enemy has done. The wars that we need to be fighting are the ones we start by going after principalities and every high thing that exalts itself against the knowledge and Kingdom of God. A passive church will not win the war. It is past time in the church that we put on the full nature of Christ. Jesus is truly the Lamb of God, but He is also the Lion of Judah. In my humble opinion, we haven't seen as much of the Lion in the church as we have the Lamb. We have preached salvation by the blood to the ends of the earth, and we should and definitely will continue. But we also need to preach dominion by the throne as consistently. We have a lot of members in the body who are born again but unaware of our authority over the enemy. Satan succeeds in his battle in the earth because all his minions are on the battlefield. The spiritual activity in the realm of darkness is constant and fierce. The church must match this spiritual intensity. We cannot be quiet or silent anymore in the realm of the spirit and in the earth.

## The wars that we need to be fighting are the ones we start by going after principalities and every high thing that exalts itself against the knowledge and Kingdom of God.

At a conference, I was asked by a group of Kingdom-minded leaders about strategies to dethrone principalities over cities and nations. My response was threefold. These are not the only three answers, but these were the ones I zeroed in on. I responded that to dethrone them we must pray them out, preach them out, and buy them out! First we must seize the heavenlies by taking authority and forbidding the activity of the enemy in prayer. Then we must preach the Word of God to save, heal, and deliver the people and unlock revelation to renew their minds against the existing strongholds. Then we must have the resources to take the territory and build the infrastructure to meet and overthrow the enemy at the gates.

After I said this, it dawned on me. This was how Jesus and the early church went into territories and established the Kingdom in the Gospels and the book of Acts. Jesus and the apostles faced stiff opposition. Like them, you and I are not going to dethrone principalities without a fight. But if we fight, we will win.

> *Then one was brought to Him who was demon-possessed, blind and mute; and He healed him, so that the blind and mute man both spoke and saw. And all the multitudes were amazed and said, "Could this be the Son of David?"*
>
> *Now when the Pharisees heard it they said, "This fellow does not cast out demons except by Beelzebub, the ruler of the demons."*
>
> *But Jesus knew their thoughts, and said to them: "Every kingdom divided against itself*

> *is brought to desolation, and every city or house divided against itself will not stand. If Satan casts out Satan, he is divided against himself. How then will his kingdom stand? And if I cast out demons by Beelzebub, by whom do your sons cast them out? Therefore they shall be your judges. But if I cast out demons by the Spirit of God, surely the kingdom of God has come upon you. Or how can one enter a strong man's house and plunder his goods, unless he first binds the strong man? And then he will plunder his house. He who is not with Me is against Me, and he who does not gather with Me scatters abroad"* (Matthew 12:22-30).

Jesus said two things that got my attention. The first one was that satan's kingdom is not divided against himself. You will never see a demon cast out a demon. Number two, if Jesus cast out the demons by the Spirit of God, it is because of the superiority of another Kingdom. Jesus likens it to a strong man protecting a house and being disarmed and defeated. After defeating the strong man, you can plunder all he possesses. Jesus was announcing to them that a superior Kingdom had arrived. It is this superior Kingdom we are a part of. Our mission—plunder the enemy! We have the authority to go into enemy-held territories and dispossess the enemy.

# We are a part of a superior Kingdom.

# Our mission—plunder the enemy!

As I'm writing this book, I can strongly sense that generational strongholds over families are going to be broken. Deliverers are going to rise up within the bloodline to put an end to satan's foothold in their generation. God is waiting for someone to declare war. Like David at Ziklag, it's time to pursue! In 1 Samuel 30:1-8, we read the story of David and his men as they came to Ziklag and found the city destroyed by the Amalekites. Not only did the Amalekites destroy the city by fire, but they also kidnapped David's wives and all his men's wives and children. After crying until they could weep no more, in verse 8 David inquired of the Lord. His question was, "Shall I pursue?"

The Lord answered, "Yes, pursue!" The Lord said, "Not only will you pursue, but you shall overtake and recover all!"

I sense that the body of Christ is in a similar prophetic season to the one David found himself in. We have seen the enemy steal, kill, and destroy so much in our lives and on the earth that it could lead to total discouragement.

But the response that the Lord gave David is the same response He is speaking in my spirit. We must pursue! Much of our teaching on spiritual warfare centers on how to stand against the enemy. But God's response to David was to pursue the enemy! Don't get me wrong—there is a time to stand. But there is also a time to pursue. I believe we are in the pursuing season. We can overtake the enemy and recover all. The Bible states in Proverbs 6:31 that if the thief be found, he shall restore sevenfold!

I would like to share with you the testimony of my daughter, Eden. She was born two months premature in an emergency delivery. She was three pounds at delivery and later dropped to one pound. I was so heartbroken at the first sight of her. She was so tiny and fragile. I remembered looking at her, thinking, "How could this be?" I had seen God heal and deliver so many people in my ministry, yet my child had to be born in this very critical condition. I was so disoriented, not knowing what the future held for her. After a few hours, I decided that I needed to get out of the hospital and clear my head. So I went to get something to eat. I sat alone in the car weeping and very angry with God over my daughter.

After composing myself and eating, I went back to the hospital, only to receive worse news! They told me as soon as I walked in that the nurse had been looking for me. She came to me and told me that they tested Eden's blood and discovered a very serious blood infection and that she needed to be airlifted to Arkansas Children's Hospital for treatment. I will never forget the spot I was standing on when she spoke these words to me and ended her statement by saying, "I have to be up front with you, Mr. Pitre. This infection is sometimes fatal to preemies!"

Those words seemed to totally drain my spirit. I sat there fearful and defeated, until something supernatural happened. I heard the voice of Gloria Copeland, who has been a great influence in my life, speak to me in my spirit. It sounded so clear. She said, "Offense is how the devil steals the word!" It was quote from a passage of scripture in Mark 4. I knew exactly what she was saying to me. While I was being offended at God, the enemy was trying to take my daughter. The reason I had no faith or courage in the situation was because offense was shutting down my spirit. It was as if a supernatural jolt of energy hit my spirit and literally snatched me to my feet. I jumped up and declared, "This is over! My daughter is healed!"

I began to tell the Lord how sorry I was for being offended at Him, and He spoke to me and said, "You just got the victory!" I knew from that moment she would be okay! The helicopter came and they airlifted her to Arkansas Children's Hospital that night. But I had zero doubt that the battle had been won.

I arrived at the children's hospital the next evening. These were the words the nurse spoke to me when I arrived: "I don't know why they sent this child up here. Although she is small, she is perfectly healthy! Her blood is clear and she's fine! It will take her some time to gain the weight she needs, but when she gets to five pounds you can take her home."

After two months, Eden came home totally fine and has never had a health problem her entire life. She is now a beautiful, married 22-year-old woman to the glory to God! I don't want you to be passive anymore concerning things that the enemy has stolen from you. You can get it all back! Sometimes the battle might be intense, like it was with Eden. But you've got to grit your teeth and not allow the enemy to steal what God has given you. Fight for it!

When the children of Israel arrived at the border of the Promised Land in Numbers 13, the reason they did not enter the land was because they refused to go to war. We will pick up in verse 26 after Moses had picked twelve men from the twelve tribes of Israel and sent them to spy out and view the land of Canaan that they were to possess.

> Now they departed and came back to Moses and Aaron and all the congregation of the children of Israel in the Wilderness of Paran, at Kadesh; they brought back word to them and to all the congregation, and showed them the fruit of the land. Then they told him, and said: "We went to the land where you sent us. It truly flows with milk and honey, and this is its fruit. Nevertheless the people who dwell in the land are strong; the cities are fortified and very large; moreover we saw the

*descendants of Anak there. The Amalekites dwell in the land of the South; the Hittites, the Jebusites, and the Amorites dwell in the mountains; and the Canaanites dwell by the sea and along the banks of the Jordan."*

*Then Caleb quieted the people before Moses, and said, "Let us go up at once and take possession, for we are well able to overcome it."*

*But the men who had gone up with him said, "We are not able to go up against the people, for they are stronger than we." And they gave the children of Israel a bad report of the land which they had spied out, saying, "The land through which we have gone as spies is a land that devours its inhabitants, and all the people whom we saw in it are men of great stature. There we saw the giants (the descendants of Anak came from the giants); and we were like grasshoppers in our own sight, and so we were in their sight."*

I could spend all day writing about all the revelations and lessons to be learned from this passage. The main thing I want you to consider is the change in warfare strategy that God revealed to them. This time they were moving from defending to possessing. There are times in warfare when you are defending against the schemes and attacks of the enemy. In those times you must stand and resist. Then there are times when God commands you to go and possess. In those times, you must pursue and attack. It was the possessing warfare mentality that the children of Israel refused to embody. They were too fearful for war. The giants were in the land, along with other nations, and they simply refused to go to war for their promise.

# If you will take your authority and climb into the heavenlies and enforce it, there is not anything that the enemy can do about it except flee!

This is still so true thousands of years later. So many people are not seeing the promises in their life because they won't go into spiritual war to possess them. Even though the children of Israel were sent to possess a physical land that had physical enemies, the Bible declares it was the spiritual and psychological warfare that defeated them. They lost the battle before even lifting a sword because of fear. The end result of all spiritual warfare is to produce fear and doubt in you! They lost the battle mentally and spiritually before they ever engaged the battle physically. What they did not understand was that these were principalities and powers in another realm that caused them to cower in fear and convinced them they were just grasshoppers.

Listen, beloved, if you are going to live out God's plan for your life and possess the promises He has for you, you're going to have to go to war for it! Satan and his kingdom are determined to keep you out! But God and His Kingdom are determined to bring you in. The good news is, if you will take your authority and climb into the heavenlies and enforce it, there is not anything that the enemy can do about it except flee! It's time to go on the offensive and make a declaration of war, and let every demon in hell know that you're coming to get your stuff!

# CHAPTER 10

# DECREE IT AND YOU WILL SEE IT

**A**s I stated earlier, it is crucial that we move beyond defending to possessing! I believe this will be the shift that the church will move into in this new era. We must realize that the ultimate reason for our authority is to take territory and not just defend territory! Jesus used His authority to take, more than He used it to defend. He would go into a city or town and drive the enemy out. Acts 10:38 says, *"How God anointed Jesus of Nazareth with the Holy Spirit and with power, who went about doing good and healing all who were oppressed by the devil, for God was with Him."*

We have been given authority to destroy the works of the devil, not just to stop the devil from destroying our works. We must make our authority offensive. Our authority is supposed to be weaponized. Matthew 11:12 says, *"And from the days of John the Baptist until now the kingdom of heaven suffers violence, and the violent take it by force."* The Kingdom is supposed to be forcefully advancing in the earth despite the enemy's resistance. As it was in the days of John and Jesus, so it is with us. First John 5:19 reads, *"We know that we are of God, and the whole world lies under the sway of the wicked one."* This is why enforcing our authority is so paramount. The whole world is under the influence of the wicked one, and we are pushing and advancing against the sway. But there is so much authority in God that no matter what strongholds the enemy has, we can destroy them.

# There is so much authority in God that no matter what strongholds the enemy has, we can destroy them.

There are two scriptures that I would like to dive into, which really demonstrate just how amazing the authority of God is in the earth. In Hebrews 11, there is a scripture that is absolutely mind boggling. Hebrews 11:3 says, *"By faith we understand that the worlds were framed by the word of God, so that the things which are seen were not made of things which are visible."* The word *worlds* is the Greek word *aion,* and it means "ages" instead of physical worlds or planet. This scripture reveals that when we look throughout the ages of time and see the things that happened in those ages, there is nothing in the natural that can take credit for those things happening. The word of God caused it all! Wow! When God speaks a word, He has so much authority that everything on earth must arrange itself to accommodate what God said. His word frames it!

The Bible says He does this so the things that are seen are not made of things that are visible. When you look around in the visible realm, you can see no reason for what happened to happen. God's word made it happen. This is the authority that God gave to Christ. Then Christ turned around and gave it to the church—the very authority to frame the ages! When you understand this, you understand the power of prophecy. Amos 3:7 says, *"Surely the Lord God does nothing, unless He reveals his secret to His servants the prophets."* Now you get the full revelation. God reveals to the prophets what He wants to do so that they can declare the word of the Lord in the earth, releasing the authority to cause that word to come to pass. The moment you speak the word of the Lord, things start happening in another realm to bring it to pass.

Sometimes the Lord speaks for the moment, and sometimes He speaks for a millennium. But whatever He says, if it takes minutes, hours, days, weeks, months, or even years, it is going to come into manifestation in the earth realm. This is so powerful. When a word is released, there is nothing in the visible world that can stop it, because nothing in the visible world caused it. Therefore, God can prophesy things thousands of years in advance, and yet they happen right on time. It is because of the authority of His words. The earth realm must submit!

It's so important that you speak the things that God has put in your heart. The moment you start proclaiming is the moment He starts framing. This how we are going to revolutionize families, cities, and nations. We have to use our authority to frame things the way God designed them to be. This is how we take by force. It's a spiritual takeover. We must use the Word like a creative force. That's what the whole chapter of Hebrews 11 is about. Also, Job 22:28: *"You will also declare a thing, and it will be established for you; so light will shine on your ways."* Once again, this shows us that the moment you speak the Word of God, the power to establish that word is released immediately in another realm to bring it into manifestation in its appointed time. If you speak it, it will be established for you. This is the highest use of our authority—to become co-creators with the Lord. To bring His will into manifestation in the earth.

## When you get a word from the Lord, you just received your future in waiting.

I want to highlight Hebrews 11:3 as the most important factor in releasing your authority over the enemy and seeing things manifest in your life. That is, you must first get a word from the Lord! You can't go to war without a word, and you certainly can't decree what you haven't heard. But when you get a word from the Lord, you just received your future in waiting, and if you decree it, you will see it.

There is another revelation that I would like to discuss with you concerning the authority to decree and bring things into manifestation. It's found in James 3:5-6:

> *Even so the tongue is a little member and boasts great things. See how great a forest a little fire kindles! And the tongue is a fire, a world of iniquity. The tongue is so set among our members that it defiles the whole body, and sets on fire the course of nature; and it is set on fire by hell.*

This scripture highlights just how much authority words have when they are not used properly. A whole forest can be burned down by one little spark of fire. The tongue is so set in our bodies that it defiles the whole body physically and spiritually. Everything enters your body through the mouth. And most things enter your life because of what you speak. It says the tongue sets on fire the course of nature, or existence. This means that words cause things to come into existence. This is crucial to understand. God gave humankind so much authority that the things we say start the manifestation process of things coming into existence. Why is this? Because the spirit realm is literally activated and released by the words of human beings. Demons as well as angels are listening and responding to the words we speak. Therefore, words can release a deluge of demonic or angelic activity when spoken.

But as I stated earlier, the focus of this chapter is not focused on the enemy and what he's doing. Rather, the focus is on our authority to activate spiritual activity to bring things into manifestation. With that in mind, think about this. God wants to use your mouth to be the source to bring things into existence. You must realize that the words you speak start the wheels of nature into motion for good or bad. I believe that this is why Jesus said in John 12:49, *"For I have not spoken on My own authority; but the Father who sent Me gave Me a command, what I should say and what I should speak."* Jesus said that He was so mindful to only say what the Father commanded Him to say because He understood the authority of His words. He knew that He would set the wheels of manifestation into motion based on what He said.

When the church understands this revelation and accepts this responsibility with the seriousness Jesus did, we will begin to see amazing things manifest in the earth. The fact is, many of us cannot be trusted with great assignments within the Kingdom of God because we are too reckless with our mouths. We release both the blessing and the curse from the same mouth. We activate as many demons as we do angels because of a lack of knowledge about authority. But I believe a there is a generation of believers on planet earth who are ready to function at this highest level of authority. We are finally realizing our Kingdom mandate! When we look at the calamities in the lives of the people around us, God is needing someone to change their existence. Someone who will use their authority to speak into it, starting the chain of events to change it. That's what intercession is! It means to go between or intervene on behalf of another. You must have the kind of faith to believe that when you open your mouth, the wheels start turning and what you declare is on its way into existence.

When you start to bring this type of revelation to the forefront, inevitably you will have people dispute it and declare you are trying to be God and no human being has the authority to call things into existence by their words. And they are partly correct. No human being has the authority to do it. However, human beings have been given the authority to do it by God. Remember, it's His authority—not ours. We only possess it by virtue of being in Him, and He delegated His authority to the church, which is His body. This makes perfect sense when you have a revelation of the spirit realm. The Holy Spirit, satan, angels, and demons are the entities that work to influence the hearts, minds, and decisions of humankind. When God gives you a thought, idea, or word, He is giving you His will, and He wants it manifested in the earth. He needs someone to agree with Him in the earth, because He does not override human wills. Therefore, He is always searching for someone in the earth who will speak in agreement with Him.

# When God gives you a thought, idea, or word, He is giving you His will.

I was teaching on this particular revelation one day and was confronted by a gentleman who told me, "God doesn't need anybody to agree with Him in order to do what He wants to do." He further stated that God was in control of everything and could do whatever He wanted. I shared with Him that God is *not always in control!* But He really wants to be. However, He is not always allowed to be. Much of the confusion about this fact comes from the inability to separate God's omnipotence from God's order. It is very true that God is sovereign and all-powerful. And should He desire to do something in the earth, no man or thing could stop Him. But it is also true that this omnipotent and sovereign God gave man dominion over the earth and chose to rule through mankind. Mankind didn't take control from God, God delegated authority over the earth to mankind. If God were in control of the whole earth, He would've slapped the fruit out of Adam's hand and kicked the serpent out of the garden like He did when He kicked lucifer from heaven, and the earth wouldn't be in this chaos to begin with! And if He could do whatever He wanted to do, He would get everybody saved, healed, and delivered (see 2 Peter 3:9). Then I ministered on a passage in Mark 6 that settled the issue. In Mark 6:1-6, the scripture declares:

> *Then He went out from there and came to His own country, and His disciples followed Him. And when the Sabbath had come, He began to teach in the synagogue. And many hearing Him were astonished, saying, "Where did this Man get these things? And what wisdom is this which is given to Him, that such mighty works are performed by His hands! Is this not the carpenter, the Son of Mary, and brother of James, Joses, Judas, and Simon? And are not His sisters here with us?" So they were offended at Him.*
>
> *But Jesus said to them, "A prophet is not without honor except in his own country, among his own relatives, and in his own house." Now He could do no mighty work there, except that He laid His hands on a few sick people and healed them. And He marveled because of their unbelief. Then He went about the villages in a circuit, teaching.*

This proves to us that God is not in control, and neither can He do whatever He wants to. If there was ever a place that Jesus wanted to perform mighty miracles and heal everyone, it would be in His own hometown of Nazareth. But because of their unbelief, the Bible says

He could not do many miracles. Not that He would not. He could not, because they were offended at His authority. I want to clarify this to make us aware of the fact that the Father needs our faith and agreement in the earth to bring His will to pass. As we go forward with this mandate, let us realize the mighty authority that we have to set things into motion in the earth with our words.

This is one of the primary ways that the Kingdom of Heaven comes to earth. "Thy Kingdom come" is one of the mandates given to the church. Jesus told us to pray to that end in Matthew 6:9-13:

> *In this manner, therefore, pray: Our Father in heaven, hallowed be Your name. Your kingdom come. Your will be done on earth as it is in heaven. Give us this day our daily bread. And forgive us our debts, as we forgive our debtors. And do not lead us into temptation, but deliver us from the evil one. For Yours is the kingdom and the power and the glory forever. Amen.*

As Jesus states in this verse, if the Kingdom is going to come, we need a Heaven-to-earth connection. That's our assignment! When I think about all the ways that Heaven came to earth in the Bible, I'm convinced that we are under-utilizing the potential of our authority. I see so many realms of authority demonstrated through Jesus and in the Word that it is mind-boggling. Most of it occurred with a decree or word spoken.

When I say realms of authority, I mean that this authority is not to just to heal the sick and cast out devils. This authority affects many other things. There are numerous passages in the Bible that address God's authority over nature and the earth. In the Old Covenant, you had miracles and displays of authority that included parting the Red Sea, the sun standing still, Jericho's walls falling, rain being withheld by Elijah, an axe head swimming, and even walking through fiery furnaces. There are too many to mention. But the point is that almost all of them were God working in connection with somebody in the earth to manifest His authority. Even all of Jesus' miracles and displays of authority were God working with and through Him.

If authority is released through words, God needs somebody to speak. When you say what God says, your words become decrees or laws! When the law of God is spoken, all of creation must bow to that law, and everything in the realm of the spirit has to submit. The key is to wait for a word from God and then speak it. Jesus did this numerous times as He functioned in the realm of authority on earth. The first is found in John 2:1-11:

> *On the third day there was a wedding in Cana of Galilee, and the mother of Jesus was there. Now both Jesus and His disciples were invited to the wedding. And when they ran out of wine, the mother of Jesus said to Him, "They have no wine."*

*Jesus said to her, "Woman, what does your concern have to do with Me? My hour has not yet come."*

*His mother said to the servants, "Whatever He says to you, do it."*

*Now there were set there six waterpots of stone, according to the manner of purification of the Jews, containing twenty or thirty gallons apiece. Jesus said to them, "Fill the waterpots with water." And they filled them up to the brim. And He said to them, "Draw some out now, and take it to the master of the feast." And they took it. When the master of the feast had tasted the water that was made wine, and did not know where it came from (but the servants who had drawn the water knew), the master of the feast called the bridegroom. And he said to him, "Every man at the beginning sets out the good wine, and when the guests have well drunk, then the inferior. You have kept the good wine until now!"*

*This beginning of signs Jesus did in Cana of Galilee, and manifested His glory; and His disciples believed in Him.*

This miracle was so amazing because Jesus didn't do anything to the wine. He didn't touch it, mix it, or drink it. He just said, "Draw it out and take it to the master of the feast." I heard an old preacher say, "Somewhere between the dip and the sip, the water was turned to wine!" My God! That authority is still available today. Take some time and just meditate on all the miracles that Jesus performed with winds, trees, fish, and people. Jesus even said that if you believe, a mountain can be removed (see Matthew 17:20).

I bring up these instances because many of us are faced with situations all the time, which we never release our authority to confront. I often wonder what would happen with high winds, floods, tornadoes, hurricanes, and tsunamis if the body of Christ rose up with one voice and all spoke to it! I believe we would see the greatest miracles the earth has witnessed since Jesus on a consistent basis. Jesus said:

> *Later He appeared to the eleven as they sat at the table; and He rebuked their unbelief and hardness of heart, because they did not believe those who had seen Him after He had risen. And He said to them, "Go into all the world and preach the gospel to every creature. He who believes and is baptized will be saved; but he who does not believe will be condemned. And these signs will follow those who believe: In My name they will cast out demons; they will speak with new tongues; they will take up serpents; and if they drink anything deadly, it will by no means hurt*

*them; they will lay hands on the sick, and they will recover"* (Mark 16:14-18).

I believe the casting out of devils in this passage speaks to a broader, corporate level of engagement. I believe it also refers to corporate exercising of our dominion over families, cities, regions, and nations. Of course, it also means individuals. However, I believe our assignment as the collective body is to shift into a greater realm of authority. Jesus said in Matthew 18:19, *"Again I say to you that if two of you agree on earth concerning anything that they ask, it will be done for them by My Father in heaven."* This is the ultimate way to extend our authority—through agreement. The body of Christ linking together in decrees, intercession, and assignments is the way the Father designed the Kingdom to manifest in its fullness. As Jesus illustrated through the centurion, we don't even have to be physically present for our authority to be obeyed.

## If you believe it, you will declare it; and if you declare it, He's committed to perform it!

There are so many things that the Father has spoken to you that are waiting to be made manifest. If you decree it, you will see it! Therefore, faith is essential for authority to work. *"So then faith comes by hearing, and hearing by the word of God"* (Romans 10:17). Once the word of God is spoken, do you have the faith to declare it? The Father says it for you to believe it! If you believe it, you will declare it; and if you declare it, He's committed to perform it! Let's rise up as a unified, connected body in authority and agreement, and partner with Heaven to bring the Kingdom to the earth!

# CHAPTER 11

# WINNING THE WAR

CHAPTER 16

WINNING THE WAR

As I said before, it is God's will that we experience victory every time over the enemy. And I do mean every time! Just because we lose sometimes doesn't mean we have to. Much of our defeat stems from our failure to enforce our authority.

> For this reason we also, since the day we heard it, do not cease to pray for you, and to ask that you may be filled with the knowledge of His will in all wisdom and spiritual understanding; that you may walk worthy of the Lord, fully pleasing Him, being fruitful in every good work and increasing in the knowledge of God; strengthened with all might, according to His glorious power, for all patience and longsuffering with joy; giving thanks to the Father who has qualified us to be partakers of the inheritance of the saints in the light. He has delivered us from the power of darkness and conveyed us into the kingdom of the Son of His love, in whom we have redemption through His blood, the forgiveness of sins.
>
> He is the image of the invisible God, the firstborn over all creation. For by Him all things were created that are in heaven and that are on earth, visible and invisible, whether thrones or dominions or principalities or

*powers. All things were created through Him and for Him. And He is before all things, and in Him all things consist. And He is the head of the body, the church, who is the beginning, the firstborn from the dead, that in all things He may have the preeminence* (Colossians 1:9-18).

It is incredible to think that we have been delivered from the power and authority of darkness. We are not being delivered from the power of darkness, we have already been delivered from the authority of satan and transferred into the Kingdom or authority of our God. Satan only has authority over those who are in his kingdom. This must mean that every act of the kingdom of darkness in our lives is akin to trespassing. It is legally criminal for satan to come within the borders of another Kingdom and steal, kill, and destroy its citizens. You might ask, "Why doesn't God stop him?" My answer to you is that He already has! God has already declared it to be spiritually and legally unlawful for satan to do so. He brought you into His Kingdom and declared:

*Behold, I give you the authority to trample on serpents and scorpions, and over all the power of the enemy, and nothing shall by any means hurt you. Nevertheless do not rejoice in this, that the spirits are subject to you, but rather rejoice because your names are written in heaven* (Luke 10:19-20).

Did you hear that? Jesus was speaking to His disciples even before His resurrection and told them what the enemy could not do to those who were under His authority. He told them that nothing would harm them. Grab hold of that word for you today. It's as true today as it was when He said it to His disciples. Again, I feel some of you of thinking, *If this is true, then why am I constantly being attacked and defeated?* It is because of a couple of reasons. Number one, as I said before, satan is an outlaw. He will break the law over and over again until you stop him. You have to enforce your authority. You must open your mouth and command him to stop, and then loose the angelic hosts and Spirit of God to shut the activity down! Number two, I feel another main reason we are defeated so much as believers is because we give place to the devil!

> *Therefore, putting away lying, "Let each one of you speak truth with his neighbor," for we are members of one another. "Be angry, and do not sin": do not let the sun go down on your wrath, nor give place to the devil* (Ephesians 4:25-27).

We see in these verses that the apostle Paul warns us against certain behavior and conduct, knowing that if we continue to violate God's Word concerning people and the Father, we will give place to the devil. Beloved, you must see it this way—God's Word functions as Kingdom law. The things that He has written for us to obey are not suggestions. They are actually spiritual laws. In other words, they represent the boundaries and laws that govern the behavior and conduct of the citizens in His Kingdom. These laws produce righteousness, peace, and joy in the Holy Ghost if they are followed. In fact, these laws are for your protection. As long as you remain a citizen in good standing, the King is bound to protect, provide, and take care of those within His Kingdom. Satan primarily does two things. He entices you to leave and abandon the Kingdom of God and come over to his territory, where he can have access to and control of your life. Or he allows you to stay in the Kingdom of God, yet still entices you to follow his laws instead.

## God's Word functions as Kingdom law.

It is this second deception that I see the most in the church. We are born again, but we still behave and function in many of the ways that are synonymous with the kingdom of darkness. This is where the enemy used to defeat me all the time, until I figured him out. I will never forget the day the Lord spared me from a horrible accident when I was about 20 years old. I had gotten into a bad habit of speeding and was always in a rush about things. I had gotten a couple of tickets and had started to receive conviction about this, but to no avail—I just kept on doing it. Finally, one day I was driving very fast on the highway and worshiping God at the same time! Did you get that? I was worshiping God while breaking the law. Suddenly, I heard the voice of the Lord so clear that it startled me. I heard in a shouting voice, "You better slow down now, you fool!" It resounded in me so forcefully that I immediately took my foot off the gas and my car started slowing down. I believe the Lord spoke to me in this way because He knew it would get my attention, and He was right. I was being foolish by ignoring all of the promptings of the Spirit the many times He was telling me to stop speeding. It wasn't five seconds later, after slowing down, that my front right tire blew out! Now do you see what the Lord was trying to save me from?

This taught me a major lesson that day. What would have happened if I had not listened to the Spirit of God that day? God all but shouted to keep me from a horrible accident and maybe much worse. If I hadn't slowed down, there is no way that I could have controlled the car at the speed I was driving after my tire blew out. Beloved, I was already saved and serious about my walk with God, but at the same time I was putting my life in danger by ignoring laws. The Spirit of God said to me, "This is why so many of My children suffer harm. It is because they worship Me, yet they still violate and break My laws. In doing so, they give place to the devil and the curse to affect their lives."

We must stay off the enemy's territory. Satan is constantly trying to get you to stray from the borders of God's Word so that he can attack your life. Don't fall for it. As we come to the close of this book, I want to use the remainder of my time to minister to you as an individual a little more. We can't conquer nations and lose ourselves. The most important battle you must win in spiritual warfare is the battle over yourself and those in your house. Therefore, the apostle Paul admonishes us:

> Do you not know that those who run in a race all run, but one receives the prize? Run in such a way that you may obtain it. And everyone who competes for the prize is temperate in all things. Now they do it to obtain a perishable crown, but we for an imperishable crown. Therefore I run thus: not with uncertainty. Thus I fight: not as one who beats the air. But I discipline my body and bring it into subjection, lest, when I have preached to others, I myself should become disqualified (1 Corinthians 9:24-27).

We have all seen and even known people who achieved amazing accomplishments in their ministry, business, or profession but also had terrible struggles and strongholds that in many cases cost them their lives and families. Much of this comes from not securing their soul against demonic warfare. I heard one preacher phrase it as being a public success but a private failure. When God calls an individual and releases them into the earth, spiritual warfare literally starts in that person's life from the moment of conception and intensifies at and after their birth. Satan's mission is to unleash enough warfare to sabotage their purpose and destroy them as a person. We see this in the life of Jesus and many others throughout the Bible. It is no different with you and me. If you could peer into the heavenlies, you would be shocked at the amount of spiritual activity that you encounter daily.

Jesus is probably the greatest example of how to effectively defeat the enemy in spiritual warfare. In Luke 4 is a passage about an incredible encounter that Jesus had with the devil.

> *Then Jesus, being filled with the Holy Spirit, returned from the Jordan and was led by the Spirit into the wilderness, being tempted for forty days by the devil. And in those days He ate nothing, and afterward, when they had ended, He was hungry.*
>
> *And the devil said to Him, "If You are the Son of God, command this stone to become bread."*
>
> *But Jesus answered him, saying, "It is written, 'Man shall not live by bread alone, but by every word of God.'"*
>
> *Then the devil, taking Him up on a high mountain, showed Him all the kingdoms of the world in a moment of time. And the devil*

*said to Him, "All this authority I will give You, and their glory; for this has been delivered to me, and I give it to whomever I wish. Therefore, if You will worship before me, all will be Yours."*

*And Jesus answered and said to him, "Get behind Me, Satan! For it is written, 'You shall worship the Lord your God, and Him only you shall serve.'"*

*Then he brought Him to Jerusalem, set Him on the pinnacle of the temple, and said to Him, "If You are the Son of God, throw Yourself down from here. For it is written: 'He shall give His angels charge over you, to keep you,' and, 'In their hands they shall bear you up, lest you dash your foot against a stone.'"*

*And Jesus answered and said to him, "It has been said, 'You shall not tempt the Lord your God.'"*

*Now when the devil had ended every temptation, he departed from Him until an opportune time* (Luke 4:1-13).

I'm so glad that Jesus gave us the template for defeating the devil: "It is written." Every attack of the enemy is to get us to move off God's Word and His ways. Even though we experience many types of thoughts, feelings, emotions, and images, every temptation falls into three categories. First John 2:16-17 says:

*For all that is in the world—the lust of the flesh, the lust of the eyes, and the pride of life—is not of the Father but is of the world. And the world is passing away, and the lust of it; but he who does the will of God abides forever.*

All spiritual warfare against you is designed to bring to the forefront all of the pride and lust of the fallen nature. Satan is constantly scheming in the heavenlies, designing the right temptations to cause you to stumble. This why you must guard your spirit, soul, and body with the Word, like Jesus did. Proverbs 25:28 says, *"Whoever has no rule over his own spirit is like a city broken down, without walls."* Satan seeks people who have no walls built around their soul! And spiritual walls are only built by the Word of God. There is no substitute! If you're going to win the personal battle, you must use the sword of the spirit, which is the Word of God, and rule your realm!

You must also guard the enemy's access to you. Now, this is more difficult. But there is something amazingly incredible about people, places, and things. They are all made for spiritual habitation and activity. No matter where you go or who you meet, you are always in the company of spirits. Whether it be the Spirit of God, angels, or demons, you are always present with spirits— sometimes even within other people. The more mature you become spiritually, the more quickly you will be able to discern things.

I was at a birthday party one time with a large group of people. I didn't really know the person that well but attended with a family member. As I walked in, everyone was having a great time mingling with one another. I greeted a few people and then retreated to a spot to observe all the guests as they interacted. As the night went on, I began to receive all kinds of thoughts, feelings, and images in my mind that I had no reason to even be thinking about. As it kept on happening to me, I asked the Spirit of God, "Why am I thinking and feeling like this?"

The Spirit whispered back to me, "You're not thinking or feeling this way. You are picking up on the spiritual activity in this room." My mouth dropped as I pondered what the Spirit was saying to me. The rest of the night, the Spirit was constantly revealing things to me about atmospheres and the spirit realm. I left that party with a whole sermon. Beloved, it is a dangerous thing to be in the company of certain people and in certain places where satan dominates the atmosphere.

*Do not be deceived: "Evil company corrupts good habits"* (1 Corinthians 15:33).

I have often heard over the years that Jesus hung out with sinners. This is not true. Sinners hung out with Jesus! That's why they were changed by Him. I can't stress enough how important it is for you to guard your heart and mind!

> *Keep your heart with all diligence, for out of it*
> *spring the issues of life* (Proverbs 4:23).

If you're going to survive the onslaught of attacks and temptations of the enemy, you must guard your spirit and soul. You must be very diligent about it. Satan is always strategizing his next move in your life. He is always roaming about seeking for a way to devour you. First Peter 5:8 alerts us to this. Those satan is seeking to devour are the immature—those who don't understand the world of spiritual activity and who are not combat-ready.

> *But solid food belongs to those who are of full*
> *age, that is, those who by reason of use have*
> *their senses exercised to discern both good*
> *and evil* (Hebrews 5:14).

Many people lack spiritual discernment because discernment is a product of spiritual maturity. You must grow and develop in the Word and Spirit in order to develop spiritual sensitivity. No soldier could survive combat without training. My whole reason for writing this book is to equip you for victory. As you stack all these revelations on top of one another, I am convinced you will become a mighty weapon of war against the kingdom of darkness! Then, once you have become skillful in guarding your own life, you must begin to set a watch over your house!

# Once you have become skillful in guarding your own life, you must begin to set a watch over your house!

If there was ever a time to war for our families, it's now. Satan has unleashed an all-out war against the God-ordained institution of the family. Not only has satan tried to destroy the family through fatherlessness and divorce, but now he is coming after the very biological identity of our children. Satan knows that if he can destroy the family, he will destroy the mandate that God gave to humankind. It frustrates me that the church does not engage the battle more on this front. We have allowed the kingdom of darkness to legally change the definition of marriage. While much of the focus has been placed on the politics of it all, I'm not sure the church is truly aware of how we got here. Every step of this systematic unraveling has been the work of spiritual wickedness in heavenly places. The church must begin to take our place in the heavens and overthrow the governing spirits over this nation. What we see on earth is only a manifestation of what is happening in the heavens. As much as I love the church and America, we must come to the reality that we have lost much spiritual ground. But the good news is, we can reclaim it if a generation will go to war! If there is ever going to be victory in your house, there will have to be unity in your house. Jesus said:

> *Every kingdom divided against itself is brought to desolation, and every city or house divided against itself will not stand. If Satan casts out Satan, he is divided against himself. How then will his kingdom stand? And if I cast out demons by Beelzebub, by whom do your sons cast them out? Therefore they shall be your judges. But if I cast out demons by the Spirit of God, surely the kingdom of God has come upon you. Or how can one enter a strong man's house and plunder his goods, unless he first binds the strong man? And then he will plunder his house. He who is not with Me is against Me, and he who does not gather with Me scatters abroad* (Matthew 12:25-30).

Jesus declared that satan will never cast himself out. This means spirits never leave voluntarily. Once an assignment is given in the kingdom of darkness, it will be followed through. Again, that is the strength of satan's kingdom—the fact that it's not divided. I submit to you that the weakness of the Kingdom of God is that it is often divided. You cannot win the battles over your house with division. One person cannot be letting the enemy in while another person is casting him out. This why the scripture warns against being unequally yoked. It is because of the potential and probability of division. We can't protect our homes from spiritual invasion until the doors are shut. For the blessing of God to come upon your house and dominate there, a declaration in the spirit must be made. Joshua 24:15 states:

> *And if it seems evil to you to serve the Lord, choose for yourselves this day whom you will serve, whether the gods which your fathers served that were on the other side of the River, or the gods of the Amorites, in whose land you dwell. But as for me and my house, we will serve the Lord.*

Joshua was establishing the spiritual order and activity over his house. When you dedicate your life, children, marriage, or house to the Lord, it releases a realm of angelic and Holy Spirit activity to govern the house. The family becomes sanctified unto the Lord. If the unity of that covenant is kept, your house will never fall.

There has been a lot of much-needed preaching over the years on generational curses. However, there needs to be just as much, if not more, teaching on generational blessings! Don't get me wrong, generational curses are a real thing. These curses are caused by demonic assignments against families. That's why you see the manifestations of the same situations throughout the bloodline. But for every bloodline there is a deliverer within each generation who is anointed to dethrone the enemy. I pray that as you read this book, you decide to be the one! I have had a saying for many years, and I encourage you to adopt it: "No matter what runs in my family, it will leave my family once it runs into me!" Someone must take authority and raise the banner of victory through the mighty authority and blood of Christ! I'm declaring victory over you family and house. Proverbs 11:21 says, *"Though they join forces, the wicked will not go unpunished; but the posterity of the righteous will be delivered."* That's right—the seed of the righteous shall be delivered. Declare that over your children and house today!

I started this book focusing on the garden of Eden because this is still God's plan for humanity and the earth. Image, likeness, and dominion are the birthright of every human walking the planet. Satan has so stripped us of our originality that it seems foreign to us to speak and act like we were created to. When Jesus stated, *"On this rock I will build My church, and the gates of Hades shall not prevail against it"* (Matthew 16:18), He had to have foreseen this day. Like never before, the gates of hell are trying to prevail. But we are on earth for such a time as this! We could have been born at any time in human history, but God chose for us to be on the planet in this age. If you're reading this book, you are carrying something for this generation that benefits the Kingdom of Heaven on earth. If you are a minister of the gospel, you have been strategically placed in a generation when the warfare is at the greatest intensity in all of history. Paul's warnings to Timothy seem to be written as if he was talking past Timothy to us. It really seems as if he is describing our current culture. First Timothy 4:1-2 says:

> *Now the Spirit expressly says that in latter times some will depart from the faith, giving heed to deceiving spirits and doctrines of demons, speaking lies in hypocrisy, having their own conscience seared with a hot iron.*

We are in this moment! Paul is speaking about the warfare that will come in the church as the end of the age approaches. Some will depart from the faith and exchange the doctrines of truth for the doctrines of devils. Deception will be the major tool that satan will use against and within the church. In 2 Timothy 4:1-5, Paul gave a stark warning to the church:

> *I charge you therefore before God and the Lord Jesus Christ, who will judge the living and the dead at His appearing and His kingdom: Preach the word! Be ready in season and out of season. Convince, rebuke, exhort, with all longsuffering and teaching. For the time will come when they will not endure sound doctrine, but according to their own desires, because they have itching ears, they will heap up for themselves teachers; and they will turn their ears away from the truth, and*

*be turned aside to fables. But you be watchful
in all things, endure afflictions, do the work
of an evangelist, fulfill your ministry.*

---

# We are going to have to turn up the heat of our prayers and intercession if we are going to survive this onslaught of the enemy.

---

Like never before, we are seeing exactly what Paul warned us about. Paul said that spiritual warfare and activity would become so intense that deception would cause many to abandon sound doctrine. We are in desperate need of a reformation in the church. We are going to have to turn up the heat of our prayers and intercession if we are going to survive this onslaught of the enemy. Apostles, prophets, evangelists, pastors, and teachers must boldly stand on the front line and combat the deceptions of the enemy.

*For though we walk in the flesh, we do not
war according to the flesh. For the weapons of*

*our warfare are not carnal but mighty in God*
*for pulling down strongholds, casting down*
*arguments and every high thing that exalts*
*itself against the knowledge of God, bringing*
*every thought into captivity to the obedience*
*of Christ, and being ready to punish all dis-*
*obedience when your obedience is fulfilled*
(2 Corinthians 10:3-6).

As ministers of the gospel and people of faith, Paul outlined our warfare. He said that the war would be over reasoning and imaginations that exalt themselves against the knowledge of God. We are experiencing this every day on digital platforms across the world—the mixture of biblical and human reasoning and arguments. The kingdom of darkness has become so deceptive that it's hard for the immature Christian to discern. The demonic strategy is to either get you to deny the faith or to contaminate the faith with leaven. Some will do both unless the church intervenes.

*Another parable He put forth to them, saying:*
*"The kingdom of heaven is like a man who*
*sowed good seed in his field; but while men*
*slept, his enemy came and sowed tares among*
*the wheat and went his way. But when the*
*grain had sprouted and produced a crop, then*
*the tares also appeared. So the servants of the*
*owner came and said to him, 'Sir, did you not*
*sow good seed in your field? How then does*
*it have tares?' He said to them, 'An enemy*

*has done this.' The servants said to him, 'Do*
*you want us then to go and gather them up?'*
*But he said, 'No, lest while you gather up the*
*tares you also uproot the wheat with them.*
*Let both grow together until the harvest, and*
*at the time of harvest I will say to the reap-*
*ers, "First gather together the tares and bind*
*them in bundles to burn them, but gather the*
*wheat into my barn"'"* (Matthew 13:24-30).

The phrase I want to highlight is "an enemy has done this." This is spiritual warfare! The plan is for the enemy to plant his tares among the wheat in the Kingdom of Heaven, so that we cannot affect the field of the world in which we are planted. But I believe that we are in a harvest season! The Kingdom is to shine forth like never before. I still believe what the prophet Isaiah declared in Isaiah 9:6-7:

*For unto us a Child is born, unto us a Son*
*is given; and the government will be upon*
*His shoulder. And His name will be called*
*Wonderful, Counselor, Mighty God,*
*Everlasting Father, Prince of Peace. Of the*
*increase of His government and peace there*
*will be no end, upon the throne of David and*
*over His kingdom, to order it and establish*
*it with judgment and justice from that time*
*forward, even forever. The zeal of the Lord*
*of hosts will perform this.*

The assignment of Jesus is very clear. He came to earth to establish a government (Kingdom). He commanded the whole earth to repent because His Kingdom was at hand (see Matthew 4:17). Satan's desire and strategy in the earth realm has always been about one thing—global dominion and rule over the earth. He is content to let us have church as long as he keeps the rule over the planet. This is why Jesus was such a great threat—because Jesus didn't come to usher in a religious system. Jesus came to impose a Kingdom. It was the will of God that the earth would be under the governing principles of Heaven. Believers are the entity through which this new Kingdom will be established.

## Jesus didn't come to usher in a religious system. Jesus came to impose a Kingdom!

In Matthew 24:14, Jesus says, *"And this gospel of the kingdom will be preached in all the world as a witness to all the nations, and then the end will come."* There is a generation of believers arising who are not content to just go to church while the kingdom of darkness governs our lives, cities, states, and nations. We must contend in the realm of the spirit until a visible Kingdom reality is manifest in the nations of the earth. Until the body of Christ sees itself seated in heavenly places, we will never live out the glorious dominion and authority that the Father so desires for us to have.

Many of you are saying that we will not see the Kingdom in all its glory until the Second Coming of Christ and the Millennium—and you would be correct. However, Jesus said that the church would be given the assignment to establish the Kingdom on the earth in this age. Until the catching away of the church, our assignment is to occupy.

If the church comes together in one accord and takes our place and gives ourselves completely over to the assignment to rule the heavens, we will see nations changed in a day. We will see whole families shifted and delivered in a generation. We will see the kingdom of darkness brought to its knees and placed under the feet of King Jesus as the footstool it's supposed to be. Then we will see the glorious and victorious church of Christ ruling and reigning in the earth realm the way Jesus intended. Let's take back our authority!

# About Isaac Pitre

Isaac Pitre is the president of Isaac Pitre Ministries, Inc. and the leader of II Kings Global Network based in Dallas, Texas. Isaac travels globally, ministering in various conferences and Christian television networks. Isaac's greatest passion is to see the Kingdom of God manifest on earth as it is in Heaven and to see every man and woman live out their God-given identity.

# ISAAC PITRE MINISTRIES

Isaac Pitre is the President of Isaac Pitre Ministries, Inc., Founder and Apostolic overseer of Christ Nations Church, Inc., and Leader of II Kings Global Network based in Dallas, Texas. While serving in these capacities Isaac Pitre is also a singer, songwriter, producer, and noted author.

With over 30 years in full time ministry, Isaac travels throughout the nation and around the world ministering in various Conferences, Churches, Seminars, Correctional Facilities, and Christian Television Networks.

Isaac's greatest passion is to see the Kingdom of God manifest on earth as it is in Heaven. And to see every man, woman, boy, and girl live out the true identity that God created us to walk in. Isaac is married to his beautiful wife Janet; and together they travel throughout the earth preaching and manifesting the Kingdom, the Power, and the Glory of God.

www.isaacpitre.org

# YOUR
# *Prophetic*
# COMMUNITY

Sign up for **FREE** Subscription to the Destiny Image digital magazine, and get awesome content delivered directly to your inbox!

**destinyimage.com/signup**

## Sign-up for Cutting-Edge Messages that Supernaturally Empower You

- Gain valuable insights and guidance based on biblical principles
- Deepen your faith and understanding of God's plan for your life
- Receive regular updates and prophetic messages
- Connect with a community of believers who share your values and beliefs

## Experience Fresh Video Content that Strengthens Your Prophetic Inheritance

- Receive prophetic messages and insights
- Connect with a powerful tool for spiritual growth and development
- Stay connected and inspired on your faith journey

## Listen to Powerful Podcasts that Equips You for God's Presence Everyday

- Deepen your understanding of God's prophetic assignment
- Experience God's revival power throughout your day
- Learn how to grow spiritually in your walk with God

# In the Right Hands, This Book Will Change Lives!

Most of the people who need this message will not be looking for this book. To change their lives, you need to **put a copy of this book in their hands.**

Our ministry is constantly seeking methods to find the people who need this anointed message to change their lives. **Will you help us reach these people?**

**Extend this ministry by sowing 3 books, 5 books, 10 books, or more today, and become a life changer!** Your generosity will be part of catalyzing the Great Awakening that many have been prophesying and praying for.